The
MILLION-DOLLAR
DIME

A NOVELETTE

R. SCOTT RODIN

Kingdom Life Publishing

Praise for

The Million-Dollar Dime

Scott Rodin is a modern day prophet with a focus on kingdom giving that every Christian should listen to. If you haven't experienced God's promise, "Give and it shall be given unto you," read this simple book. You will never look at giving or stewardship in the same way.

> **Rich Stearns,** President of World Vision US, author of *The Hole in Our Gospel*

The Million-Dollar Dime forcefully raises the questions of "how much is enough?" and "who owns my stuff?" And yet, through Scott's mastery, these lessons are shared not in a pulpit style, but in the simple cadence of story. Thanks, Scott, for the reminder that "if all I had in life was God and a dime, that would be enough."

> **WILLIAM HIGH,** CEO, National Christian Foundation Heartland

The Million-Dollar Dime is a life-changer! Once again Scott Rodin has involved me in a story about stewardship that is grounded in scripture, proven by life experience, and filled with surprises. But buckle up, it could just be the best two hours you've ever spent reading a book about the truths of God's provision.

> **DOUGLAS K. SHAW,** Chairman/CEO, Douglas Shaw & Associates, Fundraising Counsel

The power of a well told story is extraordinary. *The Million-Dollar Dime* will take you on a journey through the lives of believers who are a lot like us. The roads they travel in this story will take you and your heart to a new destination, and you will get a glimpse of God at work in the lives of his children as they embrace what it really means to trust in him. We all want to experience a miracle, but few of us want to be in a position to need one. I encourage you to read this book and see why there are few things more meaningful than experiencing God and the story of generosity he longs to weave into our lives.

> **David Wills,** President, National Christian Foundation

The Million-Dollar Dime is a poignant reminder of the all-sufficiency and incredible provision of our Lord. It also challenges each of us as his followers to examine our own hearts as we identify with the attitudes and actions of the various personalities portrayed in this captivating story. It exhorted me to re-evaluate my own stewardship of resources that God has entrusted to me.

DOUG BURLEIGH, Former President, Young Life

The cover of this book may say this is a fictional story, but Scott uses his gift to chronicle a tale that is very true and poignant. *The Million-Dollar Dime* reveals how all of us are wrestling with our growing understanding of the stewardship of God's resources and how our combined journeys lead to a solidarity resulting in joy and the revelation of God's Kingdom. It also reveals that a choice to own and keep material possessions results in isolation. This book is not about money—it is about community!

JIM LISKE, CEO, Prison Fellowship Ministries

As a ministry, we are wrestling with what it means to live out a one-kingdom approach in the fulfillment of our mission, through total dependence on God. In *The Million-Dollar Dime,* this challenge gets personal when we are all provoked to embrace a life where truly God provides for every need. The great news is, he invites us to be part of it.

CHRIS ZAAROUR, National Director: Church and Partner Relations, Compassion Australia

Scott Rodin's challenge to the two-kingdom approach to giving will open your eyes wider to the way you see stewardship and generosity. In these pages, you'll grasp anew the joy and freedom that comes from the abundance of God's kingdom and radical, all-in giving.

BARRY H. COREY, President, Biola University

This novel by Scott Rodin addresses the concept of "God owns it all" in a format that is not "in your face" but hits our hearts with conviction, integrity, and biblical truth. This book will be a classic gift Christians give their friends to encourage their walk with the Lord. Would I be OK with God and a dime? I am not sure I'd pass that test. I encourage you to read the book and see how you might truly answer that question.

JIM WEST, Co-Founder, The Barnabas Group

How do you give people a proper and biblical view of stewardship? You encourage them to read and ponder this book. In an engaging way, this story unpacks many of the ways we view stewardship today. At the same time, it drives us to a firmly grounded biblical view and how we could appropriately respond in a way that honors God. This will be a must read for our board, our staff, and all of those who joyfully and sacrificially support our ministry.

STAN WHITE, President, Forest Home

The Million-Dollar Dime

Copyright © 2012 by R. Scott Rodin

Kingdom Life Publishing
P.O. Box 389
Colbert, WA 99005

To contact the author, write to:
R. Scott Rodin
21816 N. Buckeye Lake Lane
Colbert, WA 99005
U.S.A.

ISBN 978-0-9834727-4-2
Printed in the United States of America

20 19 18 17 16 15 14 13 12   1 2 3 4 5

This book is dedicated to Kari Kelli, whose amazing story of submission and transformation is lived out in these pages in the character of Cassie Marlowe. I am indebted to Kari's openness and transparency that has made this book possible. May we all be so committed to Christ that he is all that we need and desire.

Committed

CASSIE MARLOWE ARRIVED AT the Liberty Motel in her fifteen-year-old, army green Chevy pickup. It rattled to a stop in front of the main office. The "Lib," as it was referred to in the derelict and dangerous section of downtown Seattle, was one of several rundown monuments to the area's flourishing drug and prostitution industry. Most motels in this district were merely fronts for the perverse and soul-destroying activities that took place behind their peeling, stained brown doors. The Liberty was different.

Cassie knew the Lib well. She hopped out of her truck and made her way through the single glass door into the lobby. Waiting for her was Alastair Nicol, a tall, slender Scotsman with thick white hair and an unmistakable accent. Cassie smiled.

"Hello, Alastair. It's good to be back here. Thank you for calling."

"It's great to see you again, Cass. Thanks for coming on such short notice. There's a girl staying in room six that may need your help. She's so strung out on meth I'm not sure you can even talk to her. But she has a good heart, and she wants out."

Cassie looked down at the ground for a moment and then looked back up at Alastair. "Sounds familiar, huh?"

Alastair nodded. "When I see what the Lord has done in your life, Cassie, it gives me hope for people like Carla. That's her name, Carla Rhodes. She came here about a week ago. We had the chance to talk a few times when she was down. I know her heart is open. Cassie, she really wants out, but doesn't know how. Today she was so strung out I was afraid she'd hurt herself, so I just had to call."

"I'm glad you did, Alastair. Please don't ever hesitate to call me. That's what Esther's House is here for. You said room *six,* right?"

"Yes, and I'm sorry about that. I know that's not the room you'd prefer to revisit. But that's where she is."

"No, that's fine. I still have some of my own issues to work out there. Maybe this is part of it."

Cassie patted Alastair on the arm and with a smile she turned and left the lobby. Once outside, she walked down the line of cars parked along the façade of the Lib's row of identical motel doors. Cassie was in her mid-thirties, tall and slender with cropped blond hair and an infectious smile. Years of drug abuse left a telltale mark on her otherwise lovely face. She was both tender and tough, and she knew this neighborhood all too well. As she walked on toward room six, she passed by several of the Lib's famous yellow doors. Alastair had hand painted each one. He referred to them as "A symbol of hope in this desert of darkness." Cassie said a quiet prayer, for she knew that God was at work behind each one of them. The Lib was a place of refuge in a sea of filth.

As she approached the sixth motel door, she felt her heart race and she fought to catch her breath. She was surprised at how strong her reaction was after all these years. She inhaled deeply, said another prayer, and approached the door. She made a fist and prepared to knock, but something inside her made her stop. Cassie relaxed her hand and placed her open palm next to the small metal number six. She bowed her head, pressed her hand against the door, and reflected back on what this place meant to her.

She thought back ten years ago—when she was on the other side of the door. In her mind she saw herself as a young woman sitting on the floor with her back against a radiator that barely gave off enough heat to cut the winter chill. Her legs were pulled up to her chest, her arms wrapped around them, and her head pressed onto her knees. One lone light bulb hung from the ceiling on a long wire casting grey depressing shadows in all directions. Clothes were strewn around the floor and the *B* in the Liberty's neon sign flashed just outside her window. Police sirens and barking dogs barely muffled the sounds of her neighbors' activities. It was just before Alastair began transforming the flophouse into a place of hope, and the room stank of mildew and vomit. But Cassie had barely noticed. She was oblivious to it all.

On her bed amidst the disheveled sheets and blankets was a large, sealed plastic bag. It contained enough methamphetamine and drug paraphernalia to put her away for a long time. Cassie was not only a meth addict, she was also a dealer—a major one in this part of the dark side of Seattle's waterfront. When Cassie wasn't high she was dealing, and she had built a clientele that made her one of the Mexican mafia's best producers. Five thousand dollars a day was not uncommon, and she spent it as fast as she made it.

That day, however, everything had changed. Cassie had been driving down Carlisle Street when a police car suddenly appeared from nowhere. Before she could react, she was being pulled over. It was only a missing taillight, but the police knew her truck well and hoped they had a chance to catch her in possession.

Cassie was terrified. She threw her coat over the bag and bundled it quickly, stuffing it under the passenger's seat. As she looked in her rearview mirror, her worst fears were confirmed. The police coming toward her car had a drug-sniffing dog.

Cassie cannot explain what happened next, but somehow the dog never caught the scent of the contents of her plastic bag. With a thirty-five dollar ticket for a broken taillight, she drove on in stunned silence.

She had been given a second chance.

She drove to the Liberty and went directly to see Alastair. She had come to the motel a week earlier, and she and Alastair had talked on a few occasions. His consistent word to her was, "Cassie, if you ever want out, there is a way, there is a power, there is hope. That is what I intend this old motel to become, a place of hope." Given the minor miracle that had just occurred, she was ready to hear more.

Cassie sat down with Alastair and told him what had happened. If he knew how she could escape this life, she was ready to listen. Alastair led her through the scriptures and shared how deeply God loved her, that he had a very different plan for her life than the one she was living. Cassie made a decision that day to leave it all behind and to start a new life, but she knew her life would be in danger should she choose to walk away. The Mexican mafia only has one exit strategy for its workers. But for Cassie, there was no turning back. After praying with Alastair, she made her way to room six. She closed the door, threw her bag of paraphernalia on the bed, sat down on the floor, drew her knees up around her, and put her head in her lap to pray.

Now ten years later, Cassie was standing at that same door, praying again. She shook her head slowly as she marveled at what God had done from the moment she made that simple confession of her need for him. She reached down and touched the pocket of her Levis as her fingers easily found the small coin pocket sewn in by the manufacturer. She ran her fingers across that pocket and felt the distinct outline of a single dime. After all these years, the impression of that dime was well worn into the faded blue denim. As she touched it, she was reminded again of what it meant to her. "If you will be faithful, God will provide. He will *always* provide."

Before knocking on the door, she let her mind recall how that dime got into her pocket in the first place.

It was just a few days before she left the Liberty to move to Esther's House as a resident in their drug and alcohol rehabilitation program. She had been living her new faith for less than a week, and she was challenged by Alastair to make two commitments that would mark her journey with Christ. The first was to be a student of the Word of God. Alastair gave her a Bible and encouraged her to, "Read a Psalm everyday and then perhaps read through the book of John. Wherever you go in scripture, God will open your heart and mind and bless you, Cassie."

She soon learned he was right. She found that scripture fed her spirit in ways she never could've imagined. She decided to read one Psalm everyday, and on her ninetieth day of being clean, she read these words from Psalm 90: "Teach us to number our days, that we may gain a heart of wisdom."

The second commitment was to cultivate a generous heart. To start that, Alastair suggested that she commit to give ten percent of everything she received from this day forward back to God's work as a sign of her thankfulness for what he had done for her. "This is not a legalistic thing," he said. "In fact, God will work in your heart to instruct you in your giving. But it is a good place to start."

The second commitment was much harder than the first. Cassie had just walked away from her only source of income. She was immediately broke, absolutely penniless. Alastair provided her with enough food to get her through the week before she transferred to the program at Esther's House. But she was not used to being without money. She had to depend on Alastair or a local downtown mission for her food and a few provisions to live on. She had never been dependent on anyone, and she didn't like it.

That day she went out for a walk in the warm summer afternoon sun to face the humiliation of eating once again at the local gospel mission. The breeze picked up as she walked along. Suddenly, a one-dollar bill came rolling along the sidewalk on the energy of one particularly strong gust of wind. Delighted, Cassie reached down and grabbed it, and then looked around. Seeing no one running after to claim it, she tucked it in her pocket and thought through her options. What she would have loved to have more than anything else right then was gum. A lifetime of drug addiction had seriously damaged her saliva glands, and her mouth was always dry. She worried about how terrible her breath must have smelled. She was always chewing gum, but hadn't been able to afford it since she walked away from her "profession."

She walked across the street and into the Walgreens drug store. As she approached, the cashier recognized her and was less than pleased to see her there. In a cold tone she said, "What do you want?"

Cassie understood her reticence, but she calmly pulled the one-dollar bill out of her pocket, sat it on the counter, pressed it out carefully, and said to the cashier, "I would like ten dimes, please."

The cashier was skeptical. Everyone knew what Cassie did for a living and how much she earned peddling death on the streets just outside the drugstore's entrance. Still the cashier opened the till, counted out ten dimes, sat them on the counter, and picked up the dollar bill.

She shot back at Cassie, "Will there be anything else?" By her tone, Cassie knew she was hoping to get rid of her as quickly as possible. Cassie reached down and picked up one of the dimes. She rubbed it between her fingers, rolled it around in her hand, and felt the ribbed contour of its edge. Then she reached down and placed it deeply into the small coin pocket in her Levis. She rubbed her fingers over it to be sure it was there, and then she smiled and said to herself quietly, "This is for the Lord." She looked up at the rather surprised cashier.

"Could I have a packet of gum, please?" The cashier rang the amount on her noisy machine.

"That'll be ninety-nine cents."

Cassie sighed deeply and looked at the ninety cents remaining on the counter.

"I'm sorry, I guess I don't have enough," she said sadly. She went to reach for the change when an impatient voice behind her said, "I'll pay the difference. Here's a dime." The lady pushed by Cassie and put the required extra dime on the counter. The cashier just shook her head. Cassie picked up the gum, smiled, thanked the lady, and walked out the door. As she did, she thought to her self, "If I will be faithful, he will provide for me." It was a statement that Alastair had said to her so often, and for the first time she acknowledged that it just might be true.

The dime had remained in Cassie's pocket ever since. It had given her strength and reminded her that in all situations, as he had done faithfully every day for the past ten years, God would be her provider.

A squeal of brakes from the street behind her brought Cassie back to the present. She opened her eyes and looked up from outside door six. With renewed energy she said to herself quietly, "God will provide." She made a fist and knocked loudly on the door. A few moments later it was answered by a desperately thin, seventeen-year-old girl whose face showed all the signs of the devastation of an addiction to meth. She looked so much like Cassie did ten years ago. Cassie said a quiet prayer, looked around to see who may be watching, and then walked in and closed the door behind her.

Bondage

CARL BURNS WAS SURPRISED at how difficult it still was to make the turn onto Cypress Road and drive up the long entrance to the three-story colonial house his brother Stephen had built some ten years earlier. Carl remembered how excited Stephen was on the day that he and Pamela moved in to the gracious home overlooking Elliot Bay. It was their dream home. Stephen endured long hours of work and a tortuous travel schedule in order to finally buy the house they had talked about for so long. Scarcely three years after that joyous day, Stephen collapsed in a Memphis hotel room and was gone.

Carl motored up the circular drive and parked his Prius on the cobblestone entry as it started to rain. He ran up to the front door and was greeted by Pamela before he could knock.

"Come in quickly. What ghastly weather. It's supposed to pour all afternoon," she said ushering him in to the hallway and closing the door behind them. Pamela was a tall, striking redhead with green eyes and a sharp wit. She had studied law for two years, but chose to drop out in order to raise their three children. She never returned to law school. Carl always admired her commitment to her family, but he also sensed a deep-seated disappointment in her spirit over unfulfilled dreams. Since Stephen died, she had grown more introspective. Even her appearance was more somber and reserved.

"Thanks so much for coming in such awful weather, Carl. I know how busy you are this time of year." Pamela was sincere, although she knew her brother-in-law would have come any time she asked. Carl had felt a strong sense of responsibility to her ever since Stephen's death, and he had proven to be a very loving and faithful brother-in-law. Every November, Pamela assembled her finances and asked Carl to go through them with her, especially her decisions regarding gifts to charity. She appreciated Carl's perspective on giving and looked to him for advice. What she didn't share was Carl's commitment to the life of a faithful steward.

Stephen had left Pamela financially secure, including his business and just over one million dollars in life insurance. Over the past seven years, through careful investing and a tightfisted attitude towards spending, she had increased the amount to just over three million. Their mortgage was paid off, and she had enough now to live comfortably the rest of her life without worry. But Pamela worried, all the time.

Carl had tried on several occasions to help her deal with her deep anxiety over money and possessions. He couldn't figure out how she could have so much and still stay in such bondage to the need to have more. He so badly wanted her to be free to enjoy what she had without worrying about it running out. Today would be another opportunity to help her on that journey.

"Well, it's November in Seattle, and if bad weather kept me away, you wouldn't see me till July," Carl said laughing. "Besides, it's been too long since I've been by. How have you been, Pamela? I'm sorry it takes a financial question for us to get together. And by the way, Cheryl sends her best."

"Oh, thanks. I hope she's well. I do miss her. You two need to come by for dinner sometime soon, certainly before the holidays. And I've been okay, despite the rollercoaster stock market and that lousy land deal that my neighbor talked me into. Please talk some sense into me, Carl, and don't let me do anything that stupid again."

"How much did you invest?" Carl asked.

"Only fifty thousand! What was I thinking?" she said, throwing her hands up in the air.

"Well, I think you can survive that size of a loss. The rest of your investments should be doing quite well."

"You always look on the bright side. I can't say how much I appreciate that. It seems all I can do is focus on what I'm losing, how little I'm earning, and how quickly the money seems to be dwindling away." Pamela looked at the dining room table covered with financial statements, reports, and balance sheets.

"Stephen was always so good at all of this. I feel like it's just sand going through my fingers. If this keeps up, it won't be long before I'll be asking to move into that bedroom in your basement," she said half jokingly.

Carl could hear the worry in her voice. It didn't seem to matter how much she had. She would always find a reason to worry over it.

"Let's take a look at your financials before we start declaring bankruptcy," Carl said to her with a big smile. "Besides, we're turning that bedroom into a gym."

Pamela returned the smile, and then the two of them made a cup of tea and settled around the large mahogany dining room table. Pamela had worked for days to assemble all of her financial papers. She had them neatly arranged in stacks with yellow sticky notes identifying each pile. Over the next two hours they reviewed her income statements, investment reports, and retirement funds. When they were done, Carl reported to her that, despite her deep anxiety, she had actually added value to her overall estate in the midst of a difficult economy. The news seemed to help a little, but Carl knew her heart was still not at peace.

"Now we come to my least favorite part of this whole process. I have a stack of requests from the charities I've supported over the years. I know they're all having their big 'end of the year' push, but the requests this year are just overwhelming. How am I suppose to choose between saving abused kids, feeding the homeless, protecting the environment, building a new shelter for abandoned animals, and helping the church meet its year-end budget?"

"Why don't you start by identifying your passions? Where do you receive the greatest joy when you give?" Carl asked.

"Oh, Carl, you and your questions. We've talked about this before, and I appreciate your approach, but the truth is I really don't get any joy from supporting any of them. I know Stephen cared about all of these organizations, and I guess I support a lot of them in his memory. But my passion? My passion right now is making sure I have enough money to last me until…well to last me as long as I need it. Is that selfish?"

"There's nothing wrong with looking out for your needs, Pamela. I just wish you had a sense of joy from your giving. I think you're really missing something. You have a lot to give, probably more than you're willing to acknowledge, and you can really help a lot of organizations. But none of that matters if you're not being blessed when you give."

Pamela had heard this line of reasoning before, and while she knew that Carl was probably right, she couldn't get past her anxiety over never having enough money to really feel secure.

"Well, I'll keep working on it. But for now, I do feel obligated to respond as generously as I can. Can we just go through these and make a decision on each one?"

For the next hour, Carl and Pamela looked through appeal letters and filled out response cards according to Pamela's wishes. Most gifts were fifty to one hundred dollars. Carl doubted that she gave away more than one thousand dollars to the large stack of charities that were asking for help.

The last envelope was from Esther's House. It contained a carefully worded letter spelling out the needs of the women's shelter and its rehabilitation and recovery programs. Pamela had met

Cassie on one occasion. Carl was heavily involved in helping Esther's House raise funds, and shortly after Cassie had taken over as director, he had arranged a tour for Pamela and a few of her friends to visit the house and spend some time with Cassie. Pamela had been moved by seeing how well they ministered to so many hurting women. It was perhaps the one charity that she gave to from her own convictions. After reading the appeal, she turned the commitment form over in her hands as she contemplated what to give.

"You asked about receiving joy from my giving? Well, this is as close as I come. I really love this little ministry. Perhaps we can give them a larger gift this year."

Carl was thrilled. He may have found a path to Pamela's heart.

"Great. What has God put on your heart to give?" he asked anxiously.

Pamela grimaced a bit and shot back an answer, "I don't know what it feels like to have God lay an amount on my heart. That's just a foreign concept to me. Sorry, Carl. I guess I was thinking something like five hundred dollars, maybe more?"

"Why don't you try giving a thousand and see how it feels?" he replied.

"Painful. That's how it feels. But then again, I know they need it, so I guess this year we can go that high. Just as long as they don't count on it every year."

Carl smiled. He recalled a conversation he once had with Cassie where she asked if they might expect a five-figure gift from Pamela, given her recent visit to the house and her obvious interest in their work. "Only if you count the numbers on both sides of the decimal point," Carl replied sadly. He was pleased that Pamela had given the thousand dollars, but he could see she had done so with little real joy.

As the last check was written and the envelope sealed and stamped, Pamela sat back with a deep sigh. "Well, I'm glad that's over for another year. I can't imagine what it must be like to always be asking people for money like this." The words had scarcely left her mouth when she realized her gaffe.

"Carl, I'm so sorry. I didn't mean it to come out that way. You know I respect what you do, but I have to be honest, I wonder sometimes how you do it."

Carl had spent his entire career raising funds for nonprofit organizations. For the past eight years he had served as director of stewardship for Hands of Love International. It was there, under the mentorship of his dear friend Walter Rodgers, that he'd come to understand that his work was ministry.

Walt had opened up a whole new world to Carl. Now he saw his calling as an opportunity to be used by God to help ministry supporters develop hearts that are rich toward him. Carl and his wife, Cheryl, had worked through their own struggles with giving and had begun to experience the joy of a heart that's been set free from the bondage of ownership. During his time with Walt, he'd come to see that everything people claim as their own demands their allegiance and ultimately puts them in bondage. Carl and Cheryl had worked hard to recommit every part of their lives back to God. As they did, they slowly experienced a sense of freedom they had never known. With that freedom came the joy of generosity. Walt had referred to it as the "Third Conversion," the full submission of all we have to God's lordship.

Some days Carl felt like an evangelist, spreading the good news to their supporters that Christ came to set us free from the need to own and control. He knew what it was like to be set free from the anxiety and stress of accumulating stuff we don't need and cannot hold onto. The journey from owner to steward is the transformational journey from bondage to freedom, anxiety to peace, grasping to letting go. Over the years Carl had seen God do miraculous things in the hearts of some of the most driven people he'd ever known. Carl knew that no heart was in such bondage that it was beyond the freedom that Christ offered. Not even Pamela's.

"You know, Pamela, for me it really is a ministry. I don't see it as asking people for money. I see it as an opportunity to bring blessing into people's lives. The happiest, most joyous people I know are people who are free to give generously, and it's my privilege to give them opportunities to be blessed through giving to Hands of Love. I know you may not believe this, but this really is a great job," Carl said, praying his words might get through this time.

"I'm happy for you, Carl. And who knows," Pamela replied, "maybe someday I'll come to enjoy all this. I can tell you it would be a lot easier if I could just see my investment accounts grow a little faster. They're talking about inflation, you know. If that flares up, all of my careful planning is down the drain. It's awfully hard to give joyfully with that staring you in the face."

They rose from the table and made their way to the entry hall. Carl took his overcoat from the coat rack, but before putting it on he turned to Pamela.

"Pamela, do you think you'll ever really have enough?"

She was stung by the question. She thought carefully about her reply, and she had to admit she did not know in her heart if she could ever truly be content.

"I don't know. I would like to think so. I mean, it seems ludicrous to say that no matter how much we have we always want more. I just don't know how much is enough. I guess I'll know it when I've got it."

Carl turned and looked directly at Pamela. He reached down

and took her hand in his. "Pam, you know that I have felt a great deal of responsibility for your well-being since Stephen died. You've done an amazing job managing his business as well as your own personal affairs. I know Stephen would be incredibly proud of you. But I also know that he would want you to enjoy these years. He had a way of maintaining a loose relationship with his dependence on money. I know that drove you nuts sometimes, but you know as well as I do that somehow, in good times and lousy times, he always seemed to have an inner peace that kept him going. I know he would want the same for you. I've been careful how much I say with regard to your stress over your finances, but Pam, it really hurts me to know how much joy you're missing. I don't want to say anything to cause any friction between us, but I really want to challenge you to think and pray about how you can trust God to provide all your needs and not worry so much about your finances. Will you do that?"

Pamela slowly took her hand back and turned away. Carl prayed he had not offended her. She walked over to the dining room table and picked up a few of the papers that they had reviewed. She sat them back down and turned to Carl.

"I'll try. I know you want the best for me, and you've been very patient with my questions and concerns over the years. I was raised with such a strong sense that 'God takes care of those who take care of themselves' that it's just hard for me to let go and trust that he'll provide. I guess I feel that it's my job to put away the money I need to take care of myself. When I feel like that's not enough, I worry that I might be letting God down. Does that make sense?"

Carl was thankful for the open door to discuss this more deeply. "It sounds logical, but Pam, I just don't think it's biblical. It's not like God is asking us to lie around in a hammock and just let him take care of our every need. But one of the greatest lessons I've learned over the past five years is that if our focus is on being faithful and obedient to the values of God's kingdom, we really can trust him to provide our needs."

"Values? Like what?"

"Well, I guess there are five or so that have guided me in my own transition. Things like 'we are stewards not owners,' 'we can't out-give God,' 'we should be outrageously generous givers because we were created in the image of an outrageously giving God,' 'generosity sets us free,' and 'he will always provide for us—always,'" Carl replied.

"Oh yes, and one more," he continued. "No matter how much we think we have or don't have, we have enough."

"So making money is sinful?" Pamela asked sharply.

"No, but the insatiable desire to always have to make more is absolute bondage. It's only when we understand that we have enough that we're free to be used by God to do his work. For some people, that means being successful in earning more, but even then it's from a heart that's already full. It's the heart that matters, Pamela, not the bottom line," Carl replied.

"So you're telling me that I have enough, that I should be content with what I have now," Pamela replied flatly.

"Actually, it's a little harder than that. What I'm saying is that 'enough' may be substantially *less* than what you have now," Carl said preparing himself for Pamela's reaction.

"I'm sorry Carl, that's more than I can handle right now," Pamela said throwing her hands in the air.

Carl was concerned that he had pushed too far, but he was deeply grateful for the opportunity to finally put some of these issues on the table. He prayed for wisdom and then replied, "I know I'm pushing you a lot, and I would just ask you to spend some time thinking and praying about how you define 'enough' and what it means to trust God to provide your needs. Then I'll get out of your hair."

"I'm glad you're in my hair. Carl, you know how much I care about you and Cheryl, and I know you're probably right in a lot of what you say. I just have a long way to go before I can begin thinking like that," she replied.

Carl left it at that, and Pamela promised to continue thinking and praying about what they had discussed. As Carl headed out to his car, he thanked God for Pamela's openness.

"Help her on her journey, Lord."

Scarcity

ON THE OPPOSITE END of downtown Seattle, away from the dangerous streets that surrounded the Liberty Motel, was the sprawling, upper-middle-class suburb of River Haven. At the center, safely removed from the urban realities of city life, was the First Church of River Haven. The impressive brick and glass structure boasted a steeple that could be seen from almost anywhere in the city. It's non-denominational roots made it attractive for a broad variety of suburbanites, and over the years it had known a modest degree of growth.

Six years ago, the church hired Aaron Winters as its pastor. Aaron had an athlete's build and a politician's smile. He was a handsome man with a gregarious confidence indicative of a young, enthusiastic preacher. The church was certain he would double the size the congregation in no time. When he came, church membership was around six hundred. Six years later, it had barely reached six hundred and fifty. Despite outreach programs, a new seeker friendly worship style, and even a renovation to the church to add a welcome center, the First Church of River Haven had hit a plateau. What made matters worse was its constant financial shortfalls. Every October, the church found itself looking back on a meager summer offering and ahead to the end of the year, anticipating a significant deficit. Special year-end appeals and personal visits to its wealthier members helped them avoid disaster, but Aaron knew the problems were increasing. He always feared there would come a year when the gap could not be closed.

It appeared that year had come. Aaron powered down his laptop, shut off his desk light, grabbed the thick file on his desk labeled "Stewardship Committee," and headed out the door. He had the look of a man struggling under an enormous burden. He would meet with his faithful little stewardship committee and, as they had in the past, try to figure out why giving was so low and what they would need to do to make up the difference in just a few short weeks.

This year the deficit was the largest they'd ever faced. On top of that they were experiencing their third straight year of decline in membership. It wasn't large, only about thirty members, but the trend was deeply troubling. Aaron could not figure out how they had gotten here. People seemed to respond well to his preaching. They had programs for every possible age group and demographic. The church had a good reputation in the community, and there were certainly enough wealthy members to fund their annual budget and then some.

Aaron looked out across the courtyard and saw his committee gathering in a Sunday school room. He could tell by their countenance they were struggling with the same questions.

"Lord, how did we get here and how do we get out? We need help, Lord," he prayed as he walked across the courtyard and prepared to join them.

Carl had returned home after his visit with Pamela and shared his discussion with Cheryl.

"That's amazing, dear. You've wanted to have that conversation with her for so long. Maybe God is really opening a door," Cheryl said.

"I think he is. I just hope I didn't push her too hard," Carl replied.

Cheryl noted the concern in his voice.

"You were faithful, and God will provide," she said with a reassuring smile.

Carl was so deeply grateful for her faith and support. He thought about the journey they had been on for the past five years. He recalled with regret how often he had shrunk back from the hard decisions they faced as they sought to be faithful to the commitment to be godly stewards of every area of life. It was Cheryl who lovingly urged him along. Step by step they had restructured their lives in order to be more faithful stewards and generous givers. Carl looked at Cheryl and thanked God again for such a faithful partner.

"You're right, as usual. I need to get going. Aaron Winters asked me to come and say a few words to the stewardship committee over at River Haven."

"I can't believe *that* will do any good," Cheryl said in a surprisingly flippant tone. She quickly followed up with, "I'm sorry. That was a lousy thing to say. I just don't see much change happening at that church."

"I'm not sure I do either, but I heard someone say one time that if we are faithful, God will provide," Carl said with a big grin.

"Touché," Cheryl replied with a laugh.

Carl arrived at River Haven to find the stewardship committee deeply embroiled in a conversation about the church deficit. He stood quietly and observed for a moment before anyone noticed he'd come in the room. Carl and Cheryl had attended here for nearly ten years, but as they continued on their own stewardship journey, it became clear that they felt called to worship and serve a community that was more closely tied to the life and considerable needs of the city. They had made a painful departure about two years ago but maintained good relationships with their friends and the pastoral leadership at the church. Even so, Carl was surprised when Aaron called him and asked him to visit the committee.

Carl recognized all of the members of the committee. The chair was Tom Link, a broad-chested, earthy man in his seventies who had made his living farming wheat in eastern Washington. He and his wife, Bernice, had retired and moved to the west side to be closer to their grandkids. He had been in leadership at the church for as long as Carl could remember. Tom was usually serious, but Carl could always find a way to get him to reveal his big, toothy smile. Tom and Aaron had not always seen eye to eye, but Aaron appreciated how seriously he took the job. Unfortunately over the past few years, under Tom's leadership, stewardship in the church had become a regimented, program driven obligation.

The other committee members were a cross-section of the church's demographics: Jeannie Rice, a retired schoolteacher, Peter Beddoe, an insurance adjuster and city council member, Jack Post, a local commercial realtor, and Rebecca Fletcher, who owned the Christian bookstore across the street from the church. They were all good people who meant well, but Carl knew each one well enough to know that they were all stuck in the old way of thinking about stewardship and giving—a "two kingdom" way of giving, as Walt would have put it. He could hear it in their conversation.

"People are just holding on to their money these days, and who can blame them?" Peter said. "Think about how many people in our congregation have lost their jobs in just this past year. You can't expect people to give generously with so much uncertainty around."

"Even so," Jack added, "don't they know their obligation is to give at least a small percentage of what they make to support the church? I mean, how do they expect us to operate if they're not willing to sacrifice a little?"

"I think we just need to find ways to cut our budget, because

I don't see any way for us to close this gap before the end of the year," Jeannie said sadly.

"That's all we do is cut," Tom said sharply. "Our budget this year is five percent smaller than last year, and we can't even make that. I don't know what's going on, but something has to change."

Sitting quietly and taking this all in was a very beleaguered looking Aaron. Somehow he felt this was all his fault. As he looked up he saw Carl. He jumped at the chance to interrupt the dialogue.

"Oh, Carl is here, great. Carl, come on in and join us. Heaven knows we need your help," Aaron said excitedly while going to greet Carl at the door.

The others seemed less enthusiastic. Tom, for one, didn't really understand why Aaron invited Carl to the meeting. He was no longer a member of the congregation, and even though Carl was a professional fundraiser, Tom just didn't see how this was going to help. But he and Carl had always worked together well, and he greeted him warmly.

"Hello, Carl, I'm glad you can be with us." Tom put out his huge right hand. Carl was always amazed at how his own hand seemed to disappear inside the old farmer's handshake.

Carl greeted the rest of the committee members, and then they all sat down to brief Carl on the situation. One by one they shared their deep concern for the lack of financial support from the members and they gave some of their own reasons why people weren't more generous. The committee had come to the conclusion that the single biggest reason for the decrease in giving was that so many people were giving to other causes and not the church. Each member shared a story of how much they are asked to give to local and national charities, and they concluded that it was this competition that was taking money out of the church coffers.

Finally, Aaron invited Carl into the conversation.

"Well, Carl, I know you've heard this before, but I think this time we're in a significantly more difficult situation. You're a professional in this area. I just thought it might help to get some input from you on any ideas you may have to help us get through this," Aaron said, turning his chair toward Carl and clearly giving him center stage.

Carl looked around the room at the faces of the committee members. He wondered how they would take the message that he brought. For a moment he thought about shrinking back and just helping them come up with a strategy to bolster year-end giving. But Cheryl's words came back to him: "Be faithful and God will be faithful." He took a deep breath and thought, *well, here we go.*

"I guess I want to start by challenging your assumption that the decrease in church giving is due to the fact that people are giving elsewhere. I learned a very hard lesson a few years back in my work for Hands of Love. I'd been raising money for over fifteen years, and all the time I had the attitude that there was only a limited amount of funds out there. That meant it was my job to be sure my organization got its fair share, even if it meant people would choose to give to us and not other causes. It sounds awful, but there was a real competitive attitude among most of the fundraisers I knew. Then someone helped me realize that I was operating with a scarcity mentality. That means I started with the assumption that there was a limited amount of resources available and there wasn't nearly enough to meet everyone's needs. So we all competed to get our share. What I was helped to see, and what took me a long time to learn, is that in God's kingdom there is no scarcity, only abundance.

"As soon as I began doing my work from an abundance mentality, everything changed. I stopped focusing on how to get *my* gift for *my* cause and started praying about how I could minister to

our supporters in ways that would help them become more faithful, generous, and joyful givers. You see, I became convinced that
God has enough resources to fund all of the ministries he calls
into existence, 'pressed down, shaken together, and overflowing.'
That was the start of a conversion I went through that's changed
my entire outlook on what it means to be a faithful steward and to
call others to do the same. Since then my work at Hands of Love
has never been the same, and God has blessed our obedience. I
don't know if that helps, but that's one thing that's on my heart to
share with you this evening." With that Carl sat back and waited
for the response.

It came quickly. Tom leaned forward and shot back at Carl,
"If God has all these resources, then why aren't we getting our
share? I mean, we have good programs, we ask people to give generously, and we even make it possible for people to give online,
which I still can't understand. Anyway, I'll ask my question again.
If there are enough resources available, why are we running such
a deficit?"

Tom's tone was a combination of accusation and frustration.
He wasn't so much challenging Carl as he was asking the larger
question as to why God hadn't blessed the church with all this
abundance. Carl chose not to respond immediately but to see
how the other members would take Tom's comments.

Aaron stepped in. "You know, Carl, I think you're exactly right.
We do seem to operate around here with a scarcity mindset. I
guess all these years of deficits have had their effect. I probably
haven't done as good a job as I should have in lifting up how
abundant our God really is. Thanks for the reminder. I guess I'd
like to hear you say more about what it looks like when you take
on this new attitude. I mean, to Tom's question, what actually has
to change in order for us to start going in a different direction?"

Before Carl could respond, Jack jumped in. "There's got to be a way to challenge people to be more generous in their giving to the church. It seems to me to be a pretty straightforward problem, and I don't know if it's more direct preaching, phone calling, or as Tom has suggested, perhaps a strongly worded letter, but somehow we need to get people to pony up—and soon."

Carl decided he had already stepped into the fray, so he might as well go all the way. "Jack, I respect your frustration, but I really don't think that letters and phone calls are the answer. I think you need to look at this as a spiritual problem and not a financial one. I can only speak from my own experience, but it wasn't until God changed my heart and my attitude toward money and possessions that I began to give more generously. I'd suggest that in place of letters and phone calls, you consider a time of prayer and fasting and a season of studying the Word of God and asking the power of the Holy Spirit to begin transforming the hearts of everyone at the church in regard to their call to be faithful stewards. I know that sounds like a long-term solution to a short-term need, but I'm confident that if you will be faithful, God will provide what you need."

This time there was no immediate response, just a tense silence. Carl realized he had risked offending Aaron with his suggestion of the need for greater spiritual leadership, so he was pleased that Aaron chose to respond.

"I'm trying to take this all in. The challenge I see is that most people in our congregation just don't want to hear me preach about money. It's hard enough to try to sneak in one or two stewardship sermons a year. I can imagine what response I would get if we called people to a time of prayer and fasting and serious study of scripture all around the topic of stewardship. I think I'd have a rebellion on my hands."

Carl decided to press the issue. "Aaron, what I'd like to have you consider is that stewardship is really just becoming a more faithful disciple of Jesus. It's really about discipleship, which, the more you look into it, is really the same as being a fully committed steward. We need to call God's people back to the two truths that God owns everything, and if we are faithful to him as generous stewards, he will provide for our every need. It was these two things, God's ownership and his sure provision, that changed my heart. That'll preach," Carl said with a smile, hoping to break a little of the tension.

It didn't work.

"So what do we do as the stewardship committee?" Rebecca asked with some frustration. "I mean, isn't it our job to run programs and events that raise money for the church? This sounds more like a ministry committee than a stewardship committee, and I'm not equipped for that."

"Neither am I," Peter replied. Others nodded their heads in agreement, and Carl knew he was on pretty thin ice.

"I think you're mostly right, Rebecca. I think this committee is called to ministry perhaps more than any other committee of the church. When we are dealing with people and their money, we are dealing with a pretty powerful spiritual force. That means we have to be ready, prepared actually, to take on this work. If you're willing to see your work as ministry and not as just running programs, I think you'll take an important step toward being used by God to transform the church," Carl said with conviction.

As he listened to Carl speak, Tom's face was turning red. He rubbed hard on a callous on his index finger. When no one responded to Carl's challenge, Tom sat forward and replied.

"You know, I think I'm a pretty generous man. Not patting myself on the back or anything, but I think overall I'm pretty generous. I've always believed that my giving, what I gave and who I gave to, was between me and God. Nobody, not the pastor or the church, had a right to tell me how much I should give or who I should give to. As I said, that's between me and God. So I guess I don't understand how were supposed to minister to people and still respect their privacy."

Everyone looked to Carl for a response. Carl knew what he wanted to say, but he realized this might be more than they wanted to hear.

"Well, Tom, you know how much I respect you, and I think you *are* a very generous man. But I don't agree with you that our giving is a private matter. In fact, I believe that Aaron should know how much every member of his congregation gives."

The words barely left Carl's lips before the groans and the body language of the committee members made it clear that they strongly disagreed. Carl chose to ignore it and continue.

"Now I agree that your giving is ultimately a decision between you and God, and no one should dictate what that amount should be. But I also believe that there may be no greater single indicator of the strength of our spiritual walk then how we give. I don't know how a pastor can effectively lead his or her people as their spiritual shepherd if he is not willing to talk with them about their relationship to money and possessions, and their freedom to be faithful stewards."

Aaron felt he needed to jump in and direct the conversation from there. "Carl, we all respect what you have done for Hands of Love, and I know you have been thinking about these issues for a long time. Obviously there are some suggestions here that are pretty hard for us to swallow, but that doesn't mean we won't chew on them all the same. We shouldn't take up any more of your time this evening, and we have some tough decisions to make. We want to thank you for coming, and I promise you we will think carefully on what you shared with us. If we asked, would you be willing to come back and talk with us more?"

Carl was surprised by the offer. "Of course. I'd be happy to come back anytime. I know I've been a little pointed this evening, but I really think you have a great opportunity to be used by God for revival here at River Haven. I just ask that you would pray about what I've shared."

That ended the meeting. Carl received cool handshakes from the committee members and was out the door. He could hear the animated conversation of committee members behind him and he wondered if anything he said had been heard or taken seriously. He said to himself as he walked to the car, "Be faithful, and God will provide."

Two hours later, Aaron was back in his office. He sat alone with only his desk lamp on, the poorly lit room matching his mood. The meeting had gone on for nearly two hours after Carl left, and it didn't end well. Tom continued to push for a "tough, no-nonsense letter" as he called it. "We just can't let these people off the hook," was his closing argument. The rest seemed to agree, although Peter and Jeannie both referred back several times to Carl's comments. Somehow they all knew that there was a lot of truth in what he said, but the urgency of the financial deficit and the total lack of spiritual preparation left them at a loss for what to do with it.

Aaron spoke as forcefully as he could for a more biblical approach, although he came up short in providing any tangible ideas of what that would look like. As the time grew late, the committee decided to take one week and pray and come back to make final decisions. In the meantime, Tom would draft his tough letter, and Aaron would develop some ideas around how the committee could provide spiritual leadership alongside their strident fundraising practices. No one left happy or satisfied.

Aaron replayed some of Carl's comments in his mind. He reached up on a shelf and pulled down a three ring binder that was labeled, "Finance Committee Report." He knew that in the back section was a list of all church members and their annual giving. Every year, the finance committee made the report available to him, and every year he made it clear that he would never read that section. He wondered what it would mean to his ministry if he knew what his people really gave.

Aaron thought back to his own life and realized how many times he had reduced his giving because of a personal crisis. Had his own pastors used his giving as a barometer, they could have made an inquiry and found out how significantly he was struggling. *I could have used some prayer and support, but no one ever knew what I was going through,* he thought. He wondered how many of his own members were struggling with significant challenges that he would never know about except by a change in their giving patterns.

For the first time in his professional career he considered opening the tab in the back of the finance committee report. But that would take more prayer.

It was getting late, and he knew that his wife, Connie, would be worried, but he had one more thing to do before he headed home. He picked up the phone and dialed.

"Hello, this is Carl."

"Carl, this is Aaron. I want to thank you for being with us tonight. I'm calling to ask if you'd be willing to come back and share more with us. We have an emergency meeting in one week. I have a feeling we're going to need to hear more of what you have to say."

On The Line

CASSIE'S FINGERS WERE GROWING numb from the cold as she pushed the metal snow shovel along the uneven sidewalk outside of Esther's House. There was only three inches, but it was heavy snow and hard to shovel. She stopped for a moment to blow on her fingers. She admired how beautiful the old house looked adorned with a coating of fresh snow.

Esther's House was built in the 1940s and reflected the style and grace of that era's architecture. Its four gabled windows looked out proudly over a broad sloping roof that provided shelter to an expansive wraparound porch. Ornately carved wooden columns propped up the roof every fifteen feet around the perimeter of the porch. During the summer, planters overflowing with flowers hung from each one. Inside were eight bedrooms, six bathrooms, an enormous dining room, two kitchens, and a living room replete with two fireplaces and a glass conservatory. There were also several meeting spaces that had been converted over time and equipped with video projection and smart boards.

The house was purchased twenty years ago by a retired couple that lovingly restored every room to its original splendor. Soon after the last renovations were completed, the husband died. Before long the widow realized the house was more than she could handle. Not wanting the house to leave the family, she decided to rent it until she could pass it on at her death, so she looked for a suitable tenant.

The ministry that became Esther's House started as a women's recovery program in the basement of a local church. The size of the ministry quickly swelled beyond the church's capacity. The executive director and board were desperately looking for a larger location. The widow saw it as a perfect match.

Just a few weeks before Cassie moved to the house as one of its first rehabilitation clients, the burgeoning ministry moved out of the church and into the gracious home. They searched for the appropriate name for the new location, one that would combine the courageous, transformational nature of the ministry with the graciousness of its new surroundings. When a board member suggested Esther's House, there was immediate agreement. It was certainly a ministry, "for such a time as this."

From the moment Cassie walked into its front parlor she fell in love with the beautiful, old manor. During her rehabilitation she had repainted rooms, torn up old carpeting, re-wallpapered three bathrooms, scrubbed every toilet and sink countless times, and even assisted an electrician with the complete rewiring of the kitchen. She probably knew the house better than anyone alive. Since taking over as the director two years ago, she was constantly making plans for continued improvements, always looking for in-kind gifts to complete the work at no cost to the budget.

Her real dream, however, was to buy it. Since moving into the home, the ministry had paid rent to the widow. Each year they asked her for a right of first refusal should she decide to sell. She assured them that if no family member wanted it at her death she would simply give it to Esther's House, there would be no need to buy it. Cassie was always uncomfortable with that reply, but she trusted God to provide their needs in every situation.

Three weeks ago, the day before the fall board meeting, Cassie got word that the widow had died. She spoke with the attorney handling the estate, and he told her the woman's only daughter had shown some interest in the house. Cassie waited day by day to learn what the daughter intended and what it might mean for their ministry.

As she continued warming her fingers and enjoying the sun sparkling from a million tiny crystals across the south gables of the house, she was startled by the voice of the postman, Frank, who had followed her single, shovel-wide path up to the front steps of the house.

"Morning, Cassie. Pretty early for snow," Frank said as his words turned to frosty clouds in the air. "Here's your mail. Looks like there's an important one in there."

"I love the snow, Frank, but I'd also love a snow blower," she said laughing.

She flipped through the stack of mail, and sure enough, there was a registered letter from the law firm of the late widow. She quickly went inside and took off her heavy jacket, stocking hat, and gloves. She sat down at the table with the letter in front of her, and before she opened it she said a brief prayer. Her cold fingers had a hard time with the envelope, but she finally spread the letter open in front of her and began to read. As she made her way through the first paragraph, her heart began to race. By the time she finished, the message was clear. The daughter planned to liquidate the house and keep the revenue. Because of her mother's long relationship with Esther's House, the daughter was giving Cassie thirty days to buy it. The selling price was $1.2 million, *firm*.

Cassie's hands were shaking as she saw the price and that emphatic word, *firm*. Her mind began to race with options. She knew they would never be able to borrow the money given their meager cash flow. She knew of no one who could loan them that kind of money, and raising it seemed impossible. After all of the years she dreamed about buying the house, the opportunity was in front of her, but she saw no way to do it. Her eyes filled with tears, and as she reached into her pocket for a tissue, her fingers felt the circular outline of that single dime buried deep in the coin pocket of her jeans. She stopped long enough to rub her fingers around its perimeter. As she did, she said the prayer she had said a hundred times before, "If I will be obedient, God will provide my every need, always." This time, however, she struggled for the faith to believe it would actually happen.

It wasn't long before Carl's phone rang and a tearful voice on the other end shared with him the story of the letter, the ultimatum, and the price. An hour later, Carl was sitting with Cassie at the dining room table at Esther's House.

"Cassie, I'm so sorry. I know this must be a huge blow. But God is faithful, so let's discuss our options," Carl said, trying to hide his own struggling faith in such an overwhelming situation.

"I love this place, Carl. I believe that God has a plan for us to stay here, but I have to accept the fact that we might lose it. I want to believe and move forward with faith, but I don't want to assume I know God's will in every situation. Could it be that he's preparing us to move someplace else?" Cassie asked, barely able to finish the sentence.

"Yes, it could, and if that's his will, he will provide a place. But for now we have to be faithful to look at every possible option and pursue every possibility and let God bless those efforts as he sees fit. When I think of all the times he has provided for this place and this ministry, I don't think he's finished with it yet. It's amazing to me the miracles that have taken place to keep this house open. Walt shared with me a little about how he volunteered his time to help run the first campaign for Esther's House for the first major set of renovations. What was the goal?" Carl asked.

Cassie dried her tears and composed herself. "One hundred thousand dollars, an absolute fortune then."

"And God provided it, every penny. There must've been some significant supporters even back then," Carl surmised.

"Actually, that campaign was funded by literally hundreds of small gifts. I don't think we had a gift of more than five thousand. I don't know if I've told anyone this story, but if you have a minute, I'd like to tell you what happened in that campaign."

"Absolutely, I'd love to hear it."

"I had only been here a few weeks, and I was still hiding out, trying to evade my past life. I was so broke. I had to ask for everything. One Saturday, a friend of the ministry asked if there was someone who might be willing to spend the day cleaning a rental house to earn some extra money. I heard about it and jumped at the chance. I spent nine hours scrubbing toilets, clearing gunk out of grease traps, and even cleaning a chimney flue. It was the grossest work I've ever done, but at the end of the day I was given a fifty-dollar bill. It seemed like a fortune. I put the money in my pocket and decided to pray about what I should do with it. I hid it in my room and continued to pray. All I knew was, that fifty dollars was all I had in the world."

"A couple of days later, we were all asked to come to a meeting to hear about the renovation plans. At the meeting, Sarah, the founding executive director, introduced Walt to the staff and board. She told us he had volunteered to help lead us through the campaign to raise one hundred thousand dollars. So Walt stands up and starts to share about how we were going to raise this huge sum of money. I expected him to talk about mailings and events, walk-a-thons, and maybe even standing on the street corners with empty buckets looking for change. But that's not what he told us. Walt began to talk about how this campaign would be our opportunity to minister to our financial supporters. He talked about the joy of giving, about our journey to becoming more faithful stewards, about the blessing of giving, and about how wonderful it was going to be to invite all of our friends to be blessed by participating in this campaign."

Cassie paused and took a sip of her tea. As she did, Carl closed his eyes and smiled. He could see the scene unfolding in his mind. *Yep, that's just about what I would expect Walt to say,* he thought.

"Well," Cassie continued, "I have to tell you, I was shocked, stunned actually. That way of thinking about giving was completely new to me, and I felt my spirit rejoice at the idea of being blessed by giving. Walt went on to tell us that he wanted to challenge the board and the staff to be the first to be blessed by supporting the campaign. He told us that other givers would be inspired by whatever we chose to do. He reminded us that it was not about equal giving, but equal sacrifice. That's what stuck with me, *equal sacrifice.* What did that mean for someone like me who had nothing? I suddenly panicked to think that everybody in that room, all the board members and all the staff, were going to give generously and receive a wonderful blessing, and there I was with nothing to give. And then I remembered I had a fifty-dollar bill in my room.

"As soon as the meeting was over, I ran upstairs and took out the bill. I prayed and asked God how much of it I should give. I asked God to open my heart and help me know what to do. As I did, I was reminded of that first dollar I found on the first day of my walk with him. I reached down and rubbed my finger over the dime that I had kept in my jeans as a reminder of God's faithfulness. I heard the words go through my mind again, 'If you will be obedient, I will provide for your every need, always.' Then I knew what I had to do. I grabbed the fifty-dollar bill and headed downstairs.

"Walt was still saying goodbye and getting ready to leave. I waited my turn and then introduced myself to him and told him how much I appreciated his talk. I remember saying to him, 'I'm ready to give my gift if you're ready to receive it.' I know it took him by surprise. I wasn't a staff member, just a new client trying to stay clean. But he smiled, reached in his briefcase, and pulled out a response form and an envelope. I found a pen and quickly filled out the information and checked the box next to 'gift enclosed.' I remember how good that felt. Before I gave myself a chance to change my mind, I put the bill in the envelope, sealed it, turned around, and handed it back to Walt. He thanked me and he was gone.

"I suddenly realized that I'd just given away all the money I had in the world. I have to admit I was a little shocked at first. But deep in my spirit, I knew it was the right thing to do. And when I thought about the renovations and what they would mean to everyone at Esther's House, I began to experience the deepest, most profound sense of warmth and happiness and contentment I had ever known. It was unbelievable. I had just given away everything I had, and what I got back was everything I'd been looking for."

Carl sat and just slowly shook his head. "Amazing, that is an amazing story. Why haven't you told it to anyone?"

"I don't know. I guess it sounds self-serving. But that moment changed my life as much as any other. And the following week, three more small jobs came my way, and God has been providing richly for me ever since."

"So the dime in your pocket," Carl said pointing down to the white faded circle on her Levi's, "it's an indication of your commitment to give ten percent back to God?"

"That's why I first put it there, yes. But God has taught me a more profound truth. It's not about us giving ten percent of what we have to him. It's about giving *everything* we have to him. He doesn't want our ten percent, Carl; he wants *all of us*. This dime is a reminder to me that if we will be faithful and trusting, and give ourselves completely to him, he will always provide for our every need, always."

"Even just over a million dollars in thirty days?" Carl asked.

For the first time in this visit, Cassie smiled broadly. "Yes, even that."

Cassie and Carl spent the next two hours going through the list of ministry supporters for Esther's House. They talked about each one and prayed about what they might ask and what they might expect in terms of the gift toward the purchase of the house. When they got done, Carl took out his calculator and added up the column.

"If everyone on this list were to give what we would hope, it looks like we could raise just over two hundred thousand." Carl could hardly look up at Cassie.

"Are you sure that's everyone?" Cassie asked.

Carl hesitated.

"Well, no. Actually, there is one more name. I didn't put Pamela Burns on the list. I certainly expect to ask her, but I have to be honest with you, Cassie. I don't think we can expect much from her."

"She certainly has the means, doesn't she Carl?"

Carl had been careful to guard Pamela's privacy regarding her financial means, but Pamela had shared with several friends how well Stephen had provided for her. News of the size of her insurance settlement had spread, especially among the charities she supported.

Carl nodded. "But she doesn't have the heart, at least not yet."

"Pamela is the only person on our entire list who could actually write a check for a million dollars. Isn't that right?" Cassie asked pointedly.

"Yes, she is, but the fact that she *could* certainly doesn't mean there's any chance that she will. Cassie, I know what you are thinking, but I don't want you to get your hopes up. The chances of her making that gift are pretty slim."

"Kind of like a drugged-up girl from the streets giving her only money to renovate a ministry house, right?" Cassie asked with a smile.

Carl chuckled and shook his head. He knew she was right. God can do anything. But Carl saw in his mind the determined look on Pamela's face during his last visit and remembered how painful it was for her to write a check for one thousand dollars.

"Cassie, you're a woman of great faith. I give you my word. I'll ask Pamela for a gift to the campaign."

"You'll ask her for a million dollars?" Cassie pressed.

Carl sighed deeply. "I'll ask her for a million dollars."

Cassie jumped up and gave Carl a big hug. He already regretted what had just come out of his mouth, but he knew he was committed.

"What about this other two hundred thousand? How do we go about asking all these folks to support us?" Cassie asked.

"I have an idea. Cassie, you have an amazing story. I've only heard it in bits and pieces, but every time you share what God has done in your life, I'm always deeply moved, overwhelmed actually. Cassie, your testimony is a powerful tool that God can use to move the hearts of his people. So, I suggest we invite all the people on this list to a small gathering where you can read the letter, share your story, and invite them to stand with you and this ministry in its time of need."

"Wow, I'm not sure I can do that … yes, yes I can, and I will. Carl, I think you're right. It would be such a privilege to share what God has done in my life, how he's always provided. I would love to encourage others with my testimony. It's a great idea. Thank you. Just one question: Where will we hold it? I don't have a room big enough here, and we don't have enough time to rent a room or the budget to pay for it."

41

Carl got a wry smile on his face. "I've got an idea about that, too, and I'll get back to you soon. For now, I need you to write a letter of invitation and get ready to send it to everyone on this list. The invitations will need to go out by Friday. Can you do that?"

"Absolutely!"

A New Lesson

CARL SAT IN HIS office at Hands of Love playing back all that had happened over the past few days. His talk with Pamela had been frustrating, and he hoped he hadn't pushed her too far. But now, with the need at Esther's House, he was faced with the daunting challenge of asking Pamela for a gift a thousand times larger than he had ever seen her give. Carl shook his head as he thought about that upcoming conversation. And then there was the stewardship committee meeting at First Church of River Haven. What on earth could Aaron possibly want him to say in a return visit? They had brushed him off the first time, so why would they listen to him again?

In all of this, Carl was feeling completely inadequate. Even though he and Cheryl had come a long way in their journey as stewards, he realized again just how all-pervasive this transformation really was. Cassie's words kept turning over in his mind, "God doesn't want our ten percent. He wants all of us." That word "all" had to be the most challenging word in the Christian vocabulary. He had to admit that he and Cheryl had a long way to go to get to "all." It was still so easy for Carl to hang on to things he really wanted to control and not turn over to God. The biggest one he struggled with was his reputation and how it was tied to his success as the chief stewardship officer at the ministry. As he struggled with the stress he was feeling over the need at Esther's House, his talk with Pamela, and the situation at River Haven church, he realized his old nemesis of pride and his desire to have control of his reputation was rising up again.

So Carl did what he often did when he felt himself in an impossible situation. He called his mentor and dear friend, Walt.

"It's great to hear your voice, Walt. Tell me how you've been," Carl said, delighted that he had reached him on the first call.

"I've been well, Carl, and it's so good to hear from you. Tell me what God has been doing in your life since we last talked."

"Messing around considerably, like always," Carl replied with a laugh.

Walt chuckled on the other end of the line, but he knew there was a serious tone to Carl's comment.

"Walt, I could really use some advice and wisdom in a couple of situations I'm facing. Do you have a few minutes to talk?"

"I do, but I can't promise any wisdom," Walt replied in his usual humble style.

Carl proceeded to share with him his conversations with Pamela, the situation with Cassie and Esther's House, and his meeting with the stewardship committee. He shared his deep concern about asking Pamela for such a large gift, about his own lack of faith in Cassie's ability to raise the money she needed in such a short amount of time, and his feeling of inadequacy about his return visit to talk with the stewardship committee.

"I'm kind of being attacked on all fronts, having to face my own inadequacies. And everybody is looking to me for wisdom and guidance. I'm a little overwhelmed, Walt."

"I can understand that, Carl. It's a lot for anyone to shoulder. Let's take them one at a time and think through what God might be wanting from us. With Esther's House, it sounds like you've done what you can to help Cassie put together a solid plan. I like the idea of a small gathering of her most faithful supporters, and especially your suggestion that she share her full story. I think that's exactly right. Carl, you're going to have to let that one go. God is up to something, and he's used you to put together the right situation for him to work. You need to release it to him at this point and let him do what he will do. It's not up to you to have all the answers, only to be obedient and trust and then get out of his way," Walt said with a laugh. "That last part may be the toughest for you, right?"

"Yep, you've pretty well nailed it on the head. You know me too well, Walt. Okay, I will pray about letting go and believing that God's work will be carried out without my interference. That's a good word, Walt. Thanks."

"As for the stewardship committee," Walt continued, "Aaron must've heard something that really touched his spirit. I would guess that he asked you to come back without discussing it with the committee members, so you may be walking into a minefield. But I'm so proud of you, Carl, for speaking the truth into a tough situation. They need to hear what you have to say, but to let God fully use you, you're going to need to check your reputation at the door. I know these people are your friends, and there's probably some strong emotions given that you and Cheryl left that church. But you have to rise above that and pray that God will speak a clear, truthful, and honest word through you. And it doesn't matter how they respond, or if they listen at all. Your measurement of success is not their response but the level of your own obedience. We must not get those confused. I will pray for God to give you a courageous spirit and a humble heart to say what needs to be said, and then the peace of knowing you served him well regardless of the outcome."

Carl nodded quietly and soaked in everything Walt was saying to him. Courage, truth, humility, obedience, peace—those were the ingredients Carl was looking for.

"Thanks Walt, I can't tell you how helpful this is. I do appreciate your prayers; I'm going to need them. So how about this last situation? What do I tell Pamela? How do I even begin to approach this? She's never given sacrificially, and now I have to help her understand what a sacrificial gift really is," Carl said.

There was a moment of silence before Walt replied.

"Carl, let me share something with you that will probably surprise you. I learned something new not long ago that I'm still struggling with, and I'd like to invite you to struggle with me."

"Oh, great. I'm looking for advice, and you're giving me more struggles," Carl said with a laugh.

"That's exactly what I'm doing," Walt replied. "I don't want to try to figure this one out on my own, but there may be something here for your conversation with Pamela. So here goes. About three weeks ago I was giving a talk on fundraising to a group of men and women whom I highly respect. We were discussing the implications of a biblical worldview to our work and just how transformational it really is. I thought I had plumbed most of the depths of what that meant, but then I got on this topic of sacrificial giving, talking up all of its great benefits and how biblical it was. That's when I got smacked upside the face. One of my colleagues looked at me and said flatly, 'Walt, I don't think there is one single biblical thing about this idea of sacrificial giving, at least the way we've framed it.' Well, as you can imagine, I was stunned. But she went on to ask that if everything truly belongs to God, and if all we are called to do is to be stewards of his resources, and if he promises to abundantly supply all of our needs, then where is the sacrifice?"

The phone line went silent. Carl had never considered such an idea over the past five years of his stewardship journey. No such thing as sacrificial giving? That was one of his favorite topics. Several scriptures went through his mind that he'd used when he taught on this very subject. He rifled through them mentally and measured each one against Walt's comments.

"Well, that's a real shocker," Carl replied. "No such thing as sacrificial giving. I'm sitting here thinking about the scriptures I use when I talk about the importance of sacrificial giving. What about Romans 12:1-2, you know, about how our lives are to be living sacrifices?"

"That's exactly the point," Walt responded. "If our entire lives are living sacrifices, that is, if we are all-in, totally submitted to Christ, then everything we give is a holy offering, a sacrifice of love and generosity. All of our giving becomes sacrificial, not just one big gift. You see, we have used the term 'sacrifice' in a two-kingdom way. If we own the funds, and if it hurts when we give, then we have termed that 'sacrificial giving.' I'm convinced that's entirely wrong. When scripture talks about sacrificial giving, it is a one-kingdom concept where everything belongs to God and all of our giving is a holy act of worship. It is sacrifice not because we 'give until it hurts,' but because we give out of obedience and joy."

"When I think about it in terms of true stewardship and God's provision of everything, I have to admit, I think you may be right. Wow! This really changes everything," Carl replied.

"Yes, big time. I've had to go back and rethink several of my presentations, and I even asked a publisher if I could take back an article just before it was released so that I could make a correction in how I talked about this subject. Every time I come back to it, I am amazed at how rich this right understanding of sacrifice is for our work. Now I love the concept of sacrificial giving even more. Carl, can you see where this is wrong?"

"I'd obviously like to think about it a little more, but off the top of my head I can't. So what does this mean for my talk with Pamela? Somehow I think it makes it harder. Am I right?"

"Not necessarily. You need to steer clear of the problem with the two-kingdom way of thinking about sacrificial giving, which makes it sound like it is all *our* action, like *we* are the magnanimous ones making the great sacrifice. We can't out-give God. No matter what he asks of us, he always provides for our needs. So it seems to me that what Pamela needs to come to grips with is whether she really trusts God to be her provider, no matter what he asks her to do or give. I think by focusing on that issue and not the idea of her personal financial sacrifice, you actually have more to say to her that will make sense."

Carl agreed. He began putting together in his mind how he would approach it, what she might say in response, and how he could lead the discussion in a way to help her see that it really is all about our level of trust in the goodness and provision of God.

"Walt, you're right. I can see it. This is so helpful. Thank you so much. I've got to run, but I'm looking forward to getting back to you and letting you know how all three of these conversations go. Please pray especially for Cassie and Esther's House. And if you happen to have an extra million dollars lying around … "

"I'll be sure to mail it right in," Walt said with a laugh. "Blessings to you, my dear friend, and I look forward to hearing from you."

Carl hung up the phone. He could hardly wait to tell Cheryl what Walt had said. "If we are fully submitted to Christ, then all of our giving is sacrificial giving, and an act of worship." Incredible.

Ears to Hear

Thursday came, and Carl found himself distracted by the two meetings that awaited him later that evening. He got through the day at Hands of Love, but it was far from his most productive. He kept thinking about what he would say to Pamela and then the stewardship committee. Cassie had to send out the invitation letters the next day, and everything depended upon Carl and his success at these meetings this evening. He felt the weight of the responsibility on his shoulders, and he tried to internalize Walt's words to him, "It's not up to you to have all the answers, only to be obedient and trust and then get out of God's way." They were great words, but Carl was having a hard time getting them from his head to his heart.

When 4:30 PM finally came, Carl wrapped up his day and headed to the car. He called Cheryl on the way just to check in and ask again for prayer.

"Just speak from your heart, dear. God will do the rest. He's always faithful. That's the message God laid on my heart for Pamela ... and for you," Cheryl said.

Carl knew she was right, and he prayed again that God would see him through.

Pamela was waiting at the door for Carl as he walked up her front steps. It was unusual for him to call and ask for a meeting like this.

"Hi, come in and tell me what this is all about," she said somewhat apprehensively.

Carl walked in and took off his overcoat. Pamela hung it up on the coat rack, and they walked into the dining room and sat down over a cup of tea. They exchanged a little small talk before Carl got the courage to launch into the main conversation.

"Pamela, I wonder if I offended you the last time we were together?"

Pamela looked surprised at the question and gave a quick reply.

"No, Carl. Not at all. You gave me a lot to think about, and I certainly struggled with some of what you shared with me, but nothing you said offended me. I hope you haven't been stewing over that for the last week."

"I have been worried about it. You know I would never want to do anything to offend or hurt you. It's just that I feel so strongly about these issues, and I know that Stephen would have wanted you to be happy. I don't have all the answers, but I have seen a lot of people set free from the anxiety and stress that money and ownership can bring. So I guess sometimes I let my passion get the best of me. I'm so glad you weren't offended," he said with some relief.

"I know you meant the best," she continued, "but I'm a long ways from being what you want me to be. You talk a lot about this being a journey. I guess I just have a long way to go. I'm not sure I even fully agree with everything you say, but I will admit I get tired of the anxiety. I'd love to take it a little more lightly, so I'm open to listening." Then she opened the door that Carl had been praying for. "Please don't worry about ever telling me what's on your heart. I promise you'll never offend me."

Well, here goes, he thought.

"Well then, Pam, I came here to tell you something that God has laid on my heart. Actually, I came here on Cassie's behalf to ask you to consider something, something you will probably find incredible. But before I ask you that, I have another question first.

When you hear the phrase, 'God owns it all,' what does it mean to you?"

Pamela looked surprised by the question. She wrinkled up her forehead and indicated that she was not real pleased to have to answer it. She thought for a few moments, sipped more on her tea, and replied, "I guess I think it's a nice sentiment, but not very practical. Ultimately I do believe everything belongs to God. But, for a while, it also belongs to me, and I need to take care of it. Isn't that what you mean when you talk about stewardship?"

"But what if it never belongs to us, not even for a short time? What if it is always, only God's? What if we are only ever just stewards of all of God's stuff? Maybe we have some temporary ownership, like a deed to a house or money in a portfolio, but that's not real ownership. What if it's never really ours? Can you imagine that?" Carl asked carefully.

"I can try. But how does that get you to the question you came to ask me?" she asked a bit impatiently.

"If you'll indulge me, I have one more question first. I talked to Walt Rodgers earlier this week. He asked me to send along his greetings to you, by the way. We were talking about this issue of God owning everything and also about the fact that he always provides for our every need. Then Walt hit me with this pretty radical idea. He said that if it's true that God owns absolutely everything, and if he always meets all of our needs, then there is no such thing as us making a sacrificial gift. If all of our lives are submitted to Christ, then all giving is really holy, sacrificial giving. Walt called it an act of worship. You see, whatever God asks us to give, all we are doing is being stewards of what's already his. And regardless of what he asks us to give, he's promised to provide all of our needs. So there can be no real sacrifice on our part, only obedience and joyful giving. Pretty radical, huh? So tell me what you think of that," Carl said trying to hide his anxiety over how Pamela might respond.

Pamela took a deep breath and worked the tea bag in her cup with a small silver spoon bearing the emblem of the Grand Canyon on the handle. Carl could tell she was struggling with a response. He wanted to let her off the hook, but he was too curious as to what she must be thinking, so he let her ponder silently for several moments. Finally she looked up.

"I guess it's hard to argue with. All I know is it certainly *feels* like sacrifice. So, Carl, what's the big question?" she asked with a kind of determination that let Carl know he'd better get to the point.

Carl shuffled around a bit in his seat. His nervousness both surprised and unnerved Pamela, who braced herself for what he was about to say.

"Pamela, I need to tell you a brief story and then ask you to consider praying about something." Carl went on to share about the letter that Cassie had received regarding the offer to buy the house, the $1.2 million price tag, and the deadline. Pamela listened intently and was moved by the urgency of the need. However, when Carl began to talk about his discussion with Cassie and about how they might raise the money, he noticed Pamela's face turned stern and cold. He decided to go right to the point.

"Cassie and I determined that the best we could possibly hope to raise from the current supporters of Esther's House was about two hundred thousand. That leaves her a million dollars short. I suggested we hold a meeting with all of her strongest supporters. We'll share the need, but most importantly, I asked Cassie if she would tell her story. I don't think anyone has ever heard her full testimony of what God has done in her life. Because she is the director of Esther's House, I think it would be important for everyone to hear it. Then she will ask people to pray about pledges, and we'll see what God will do. Pamela, I'd like you to go with Cheryl and me to be part of that meeting."

"Of course, I'd be happy to attend, you know that. But I get a feeling that's not the big question, is it?"

"No, well, it's only part of it," Carl replied. "Pamela, there's no one we know of who cares about the ministry of Esther's House who has the capacity to write the kind of check that can allow Cassie to buy that house. No one except you. I'd like to ask you to pray about the possibility that God may lay on your heart the desire to give the rest of what they need to buy the house before the deadline."

There it was. It was out on the table.

Pamela replied, slowly and intentionally, with an air of incredulity. "You mean, give a million dollars? Seriously, Carl, is that what you're asking?"

Carl nodded. "Yes, Pamela, that's what I'm asking on Cassie's behalf. I'm not looking for an answer tonight. I'm just asking if you'll take a few days to think and pray about it. Then come with us to hear Cassie's story and be open to what God may do."

"Carl, I will pray about what God might have me do, and I will gladly come with you and Cheryl to the meeting, but I can tell you right now that it is highly unlikely that I will give a million dollars. I know it must've been tough for you to come here to ask me this, and I appreciate the fact that this seems like a pretty impossible goal in such a short amount of time, but if God is going to provide, he is going to need to raise up a lot of other people in addition to me. That size of gift is just out of the question," she said with some defiance in her voice.

"I understand, and I appreciate your willingness to pray about it and join us at the meeting. That's all I ask, Pamela. I need to get going."

"So where will this meeting be held?" Pamela asked as Carl put on his overcoat.

"Well, that's another interesting story. I'm actually leaving here to go meet with the stewardship committee at River Haven to ask them to host the meeting at the church."

"You're kidding, aren't you? River Haven? I thought they banned any outside organizations from speaking there?"

"They did, but I'm off to change their minds," Carl replied.

Pamela just raised her eyebrows and gave a look that indicated she had little faith that he would be successful.

With that, Carl was out the door and on his way to the committee meeting.

Test Me in This

THE RIVER HAVEN STEWARDSHIP Committee met promptly at seven for an emergency session. There was heaviness in the room as Aaron gave a brief devotion and prayer. Tom chaired the meeting and opened with an update on giving for the last two Sundays. The deficit had widened slightly, and there was no indication of a strong year-end surge to bail them out this year. The church carried a small reserve, but at this point it would be completely depleted just to balance the budget at the end of the year. Tom had been a champion of building that reserve as a rainy day fund, but it appeared now that they would start the new year with no reserve and a three-year trend of decreased giving.

"Well, in looking at these numbers, it's pretty clear that it's going to be tougher than ever to pull out of this by year's end. Pastor, I think it's time to get pretty aggressive on two fronts. First, I think we need to cut back any discretionary spending that's left in the budget. I know there's not much, but I think we need to go back and find every penny we can. Then I think we need to let everyone in the congregation know just what dire straits we're in and challenge them to be generous before the end of the year. This is going to take an all-out effort to keep us from swimming in red ink," Tom said to the dejected little committee.

Most heads nodded in sad agreement.

"I just don't see any other options," Pete echoed. "But I think that won't even get to the root of the problem. I mean, how do we make sure we don't end up in the same place next year? This will be three straight years of decreased giving. If we don't turn that trend around, we may face the same problem next year, and maybe with no reserve."

"Now look, we need to do everything we can to not touch that reserve," Tom said pointedly. "It's not that big to begin with, and if we eat into it now, then we are really heading in the wrong direction." He wanted to be clear that relying on the reserve was not an option, even though everyone else around the table was resigned to the fact that it would likely be their *only* option.

Aaron had sat quietly, internally grimacing at the conversation. The whole situation felt surreal to him. There were so many good things going on at River Haven. Why did they consistently find themselves in such a desperate financial situation? There was a lull in the conversation, and he knew he needed to provide spiritual direction in the midst of this crisis. He had not told the committee that he'd invited Carl to return, and he would be here within the hour.

"I think you're right, Pete," Aaron said. "Even if we fix the problem to get us through the end of the year, we're facing a larger concern, and it's a spiritual problem. I've been thinking a lot about what Carl shared with us last week. I need to do a better job equipping our people to be better stewards. I just don't know how to do that without offending everyone, and the last thing we can afford now is to upset and lose some of our better givers. I'm going to need your help figuring out how we, together, can improve the stewardship in this church. Do you agree?"

He looked around the table for both support and some ownership from his colleagues.

Several committee members offered an unenthusiastic nod, and then there was silence. Finally Tom spoke, "That's likely what we'll need to do, pastor. But with all due respect, that's for next year, and we have to face this crisis now. I'd like the committee's approval to send my letter to all the members."

Tom handed out a copy of the draft of his letter to the committee members. Then he continued.

"I think you'll see that I have put it on the line that their not stepping up to the plate with their giving has put us in this crisis. I've told them that this is our church, and we need to count on everyone to give generously to run this place. I know that sounds like a lot of business terms, but we need to start running this more like a business, especially our income stream."

Jeannie mustered the courage to speak up, "I agree with you, Tom, but I wonder if we can do a little of both at the same time. I mean, we can send out your letter, but can we add some language to try to start talking about the bigger issue of stewardship and not just focus on a one-time gift to get us through the end of the year?"

Rebecca agreed. "Yes, Jeannie, I think that's a great idea. We have to be strong in how we ask to get us through this crisis, but can we also help people think beyond the end of the year?"

"That concerns me," Jack replied. "We can't water this thing down," he said, waving Tom's letter in the air. "I agree with Tom that we need to keep our eyes on the goal and stay focused on a hard push at year's end. To do more than that might mean we don't close this gap and have to dip into that reserve."

The conversation continued like that for the next twenty minutes or so. Tom and Jack wanted a hard-nosed direct approach. Rebecca and Jeannie pushed for a broader perspective. Pete played peacemaker. In all this, Aaron just listened, growing number every minute. Suddenly, he realized Carl was about to arrive, so he broke in.

"I know this is an important decision we need to make tonight, but I do think that whatever we decide needs to be set in this larger question of how to help our congregation be better stewards in the long run. Tom, I agree that your letter will put our cards on the table and let people know where we stand. However, I think everything we do from this point on needs to encourage biblical stewardship. I still don't know how to do that. I really don't think any of us do. So, I asked Carl to come back and share little bit more with us to get our thinking going in the right direction. He'll be here in about five minutes, and I'd ask us all to be open to what he has to say to us," Aaron said, ready for the backlash.

It came.

"Pastor, I wish you would've asked us before asking Carl back," Tom retorted. "It's not that we don't respect him or what he has to say, but frankly, I don't think we can afford losing valuable time in the midst of this crisis. But since he's coming, can we agree to keep his time to no more than twenty minutes?"

"I think twenty minutes is an appropriate amount of time," Aaron replied. "And I'm sorry for not asking you first. I just felt strongly led to hear him again before we make any final decisions. Thanks for being open to what he might say."

The timing was good, because a moment later Carl arrived at the door. As he walked in he could sense the tension in the air and even picked up the fact that his presence was not warmly received. He gave a quick look to Aaron to see if they still wanted him to speak.

Aaron stood and greeted Carl with a warm smile. "Carl, good to have you here. Thanks again for giving us a little more of your time." Aaron escorted Carl to an open chair at the table. The members of the committee gave him an obligatory smile and mumbled a few words of welcome. Then Tom jumped in.

"Carl, Pastor just informed us you were coming, so we're a little unprepared. I think you should know that we're in the middle of a discussion about the right tone for the letter we plan to send to our members in order to raise the money we need before the end of the year. We'd appreciate hearing from you on that subject, but I'm afraid we're going to have to ask you to keep to a twenty minute timeframe. We need time to make this decision tonight in order to move ahead."

Carl shot a quiet prayer off and then responded, "No problem, Tom. I understand the urgency of the task you're facing, so I won't take up more time than you can allow. Aaron asked me to come back and share a little more about what it would look like for River Haven to develop a culture of giving around the biblical understanding of our call to be faithful stewards. But before I begin, let me ask you this: Throughout the year, how much do you ask your people to give?"

Tom was unhappy with the question because he knew it would take them down a different road than he wanted to go.

Jack responded, "We do a Stewardship Sunday where we ask everyone to consider a tithe, but in reality we get about two to three percent per member. I think if we could just that get closer to five percent, we'd be in good shape. Am I right?"

"Yeah, I think that's about it, Jack," Pete replied. "Maybe in this letter we can ask everyone to look at their giving for the past year and see if they can give an extra gift before the end of the year that'll get them closer to that mark."

"We have to do the math on that to see if it would really close the deficit, but that's not a bad idea," Tom replied, glad to be back on the subject of the letter.

Carl looked at Aaron and waited for him to respond. He was surprised at how quiet Aaron remained during this conversation. "Aaron, what do you believe you should be asking the people to give?" he asked directly.

Aaron shuffled nervously. Carl had put him a bit on the spot.

"Of course we would love everyone to give the full tithe," Aaron began. "But in this economy, that's just about impossible for most all of our people. I think if we could get to the five percent mark and then slowly move them up over the coming years, that'll be a huge step ahead for us," he replied with a noticeable lack of conviction in his voice.

"Okay," Carl replied. "Here's my message for the fifteen minutes I have left. I believe there's only one biblical answer to the question I asked, and it took me a long time to figure it out. In fact, I never fully figured it out. I believe scripture calls us to give everything. Not five percent, not ten percent, but one hundred percent of everything we have and everything we are. I don't think we can shrink back and ask anything less of our people."

Carl hesitated just for a moment to let that sink in, but Jack jumped in before he could continue.

"Carl, I appreciate as much as anyone the way scripture talks about being fully committed to Christ. I know the story of the rich young ruler and all the different ways that can be interpreted. And on a spiritual level, I agree with you, but I know you're not asking us to send a letter out to everyone telling them to give everything they have to the church, are you?"

Carl chose his words carefully in response, "I guess I'm not asking you to send out a letter at all unless you're willing to challenge people in their two-kingdom way of life."

"Two-kingdom what?" Rebecca asked, a little irritated.

"Our two-kingdom way of life. Let me explain briefly. Jack, you're right, scripture does call us to be fully committed to Christ. We are all familiar with Jesus' teachings on the kingdom of God. Well, we are all citizens of that kingdom, and we're called to put everything we have and everything we are under the Lordship of the head of that kingdom, Jesus Christ. That means our relationship with God, the way we view ourselves, our responsibility to love our neighbor, and our care for creation are all part of this one kingdom under one Lord. When we talk about what it means to be a faithful steward, it means being a one-kingdom disciple."

Tom tapped his foot and looked down at his watch. Carl ignored him and continued.

"I believe scripture tells us that the real abundant, joyful, and peaceful life that God has for us is found in living all of our lives as one-kingdom people. The problem is we like to keep control over things for our selves, and so we build a second kingdom where we can play the lord. All of us have these second kingdoms. Here's my confession. In my kingdom I put my time, my control over a couple of relationships, and my concern for my reputation. I still can't submit these things fully over to Christ, so I keep them in my own separate kingdom. As long as they're there, I will stew about them, worry about them, and mostly mess things up concerning them. For a lot of people, their money and possessions are in that second kingdom. They may be deeply committed Christians, but they have never been challenged to place everything before Christ and really give up control."

Carl turned to look directly at Aaron and continued.

"Aaron, as long as we allow the people in the congregation to live comfortably as two-kingdom Christians, they will never know the joy of being generous. Their giving will always be just a transfer of assets from their own kingdom to the church, and that means it will never be done with the heart of a truly generous and faithful steward. This committee will sit around year after year trying to figure out ways to entice, cajole, or even shame people into making that transfer of assets. And I'm afraid you'll be facing deficits year after year."

Carl paused for a moment and looked around the room. Most every face stared intently back at him. He had the sense that maybe, just maybe, some of this was getting through to everyone except Tom, who had picked up a piece of paper and a pencil and was fine-tuning his letter. Carl wanted to leave on a positive note, so he continued.

"My challenge to you is to consider three things. First, are you willing to be used by God to challenge people in their two-kingdom lifestyles? If you are, then I would encourage you to focus their eyes on what it means to give one hundred percent—everything—to the God who owns it all anyway. That's the whole tithe that God wants from us. And if you choose to send out a year-end letter, perhaps Malachi 3:10 might be a verse to use, if you are willing to call people to one-kingdom living. Second, are you willing to challenge yourselves in terms of your own second kingdoms? That is, are you willing to let the transformation begin with you and model for your congregation what it looks like? And finally, are you willing - as a congregation - to look at the way River Haven has built its own second kingdom?

"Let me end with a request around this third challenge. I know that you have a standing rule not to let outside groups do any fundraising events at the church. I've talked with Aaron about this, and I know that the reason is due to your concern that if people give to outside ministries they might give less to the church. I'd like to have you consider tonight that this policy reflects a two-kingdom way of thinking. Instead, what if we could encourage all of our members to develop hearts that are rich toward God, then there will be enough resources for all of God's work. I shared a little bit of that with you last time I was here. I believe if you would open up the church to allow other ministries to speak to your members, it will send a clear message that being a faithful steward is not about making sure the church gets its slice of the pie from a pool of scarce resources, but it's about God's incredible abundance that starts with helping people become one-kingdom stewards. And, yes, giving everything they have into God's hands. To that end, I'd like to make a specific request."

Carl went on to share briefly about the situation at Esther's

House and the need for a small gathering of supporters, many of which were members at River Haven.

"I'm asking if you will allow Cassie to hold a small fundraising event for Esther's House here at the church on the Tuesday before Thanksgiving. We just need a room big enough for about forty people from seven to eight-thirty in the evening. And one more thing, I would especially request that all of you attend. It would be a wonderful show of support for Cassie, and I know you will enjoy hearing her story."

Carl looked at Tom and could see clearly that he was skeptical. Still, Carl felt right about speaking the truth, and he would lay this now in God's hands.

"Tom, thank you for the time. I know you and Bernice are supporters of Esther's House, so I am praying you will be open to my request."

Tom and Bernice had been supporting Cassie for the past three years, ever since their granddaughter was found clutching to life in a meth house in Portland, Oregon. They knew very little about the devastating effects of the drug, and Cassie had become a friend and prayer supporter as they walked the long road with their granddaughter through her recovery.

"I think my twenty minutes are up. I hope some of this was helpful. Can I ask for a response from the committee to my request later tonight? Cassie needs to send out the invitations tomorrow."

"We'll talk about it and let you know, Carl," Tom replied flatly.

Aaron's heart was heavy, and yet there was something in Carl's words that gave him a spark of hope. This understanding of the two-kingdom lifestyle resonated deeply with Aaron. Scriptures started flowing to his mind that directly attacked the two-kingdom way of life. Maybe in framing the issue this way, Aaron could begin to develop a plan for leading his congregation to be one-kingdom stewards. His hope was mixed with the stark reality of how far he needed to go as River Haven's pastor, and how far the stewardship committee needed to go to make the journey with him.

"Carl, you've given us a new way to think about our work, and we're greatly appreciative. We'll be sure to get back to you on our decision regarding Esther's House. Blessings to you in your work for Hands of Love, and thanks again for coming," Aaron said escorting Carl to the door.

After the door closed behind Carl, Aaron paused for a moment to collect his thoughts. Then he turned and walked back to join his stewardship committee. There was a new sense of resolve in Aaron's heart. He couldn't see the road ahead, but he had a deep conviction that it was time to step out in faith. He looked around at the committee members, and before Tom could regain control of the direction of the meeting, he spoke.

"Friends, my heart has been moved tonight by what Carl shared with us. I have to confess I've done a poor job of really understanding what we're all facing when it comes to stewardship. I think I've underestimated the size of the task, and I've certainly gone at it pretty timidly. I need to ask your forgiveness because my timidity has made all of our jobs harder. I'd like to have us make a commitment tonight, as a committee, to change all of that. I don't know exactly what the steps are, but I think God is sending us a clear message that we need to go in a significantly new direction. And I want to begin by hosting that fundraising event for Esther's House."

Tom rubbed his face with his enormous hands, indicating his struggle with what Aaron said, but Jeannie came to his rescue.

"I agree with you, Pastor. Maybe by being so closed to outside ministries, we have closed ourselves off to what the Holy Spirit might want to do with our people," she said.

Bless you, Jeannie, Aaron thought.

The rest of the committee recognized that Aaron felt strongly about this issue, and they hesitated to disagree with him. Even Tom acquiesced.

"Okay Pastor, if you feel like this is the right thing to do, then we'll support you. But it's getting late. We need to come to a decision about this letter. From what I took away from our time with Carl, he's not so much against us sending a letter. He just wants us to be sure to use it as a way to help people be better tithers," he said in a generally conciliatory tone.

"I'm not sure that's quite it, Tom," Jack said. "I think he is challenging us to rethink the whole way we look at tithing. This one hundred percent idea is pretty radical. I have no idea how to include it in a letter. Aaron, any thoughts?"

"I can't think of the exact wording, but I think we have to get people to think beyond five or ten percent and get them to start considering that following Jesus is a one hundred percent commitment. That's a lot to do in one letter, especially when I haven't been preaching it the last seven years. But I think we have to start somewhere, and there's no better time than this," Aaron replied.

Tom pressed the issue. "Okay, so we can talk about how being fully committed to Christ should motivate us to give generously. I can buy that. I think it can still be a very strong letter and call people to a level of accountability in their tithing. I just hope it will work."

Pete added, "Well, there's no guarantee."

All during this exchange, Rebecca had been buried in her Bible, flipping pages and reading. Finally she looked up and replied, "Well, maybe there is. Carl told us to look at Malachi 3:10. Here it is, 'Bring the whole tithe into the storehouse, that there may be food in my house. Test me in this, says the LORD Almighty, and see if I will not throw open the floodgates of heaven and pour out so much blessing that you will not have room enough for it.'"

Prepared

CARL COULD HARDLY WAIT to tell Cassie the news. It was Friday morning, and he had just heard from Aaron that the River Haven stewardship committee had approved his request for Esther's House to hold their fundraising meeting there. He was not as excited to break the news to her of the outcome of his meeting with Pamela.

"Good morning, Cassie. Did I catch you before things got too busy at the house?" he asked, calling from his office at Hands of Love.

"Yes, and good morning to you. This is a great time to talk. I hope you have some good news for me," Cassie replied.

"Well, some. River Haven has agreed to host the event a week from this coming Tuesday. In addition to the people we're going to invite, I've asked for the stewardship committee to attend as well. I hope that's okay."

"That's great, Carl. Thank you so much. I'd be happy to have the committee members there. You'll have to tell me sometime how you pulled that off. So I can go ahead and send out the invitations?"

"Yes, let's get those out today. I think this is really going to work well, Cassie."

There was a little hesitation before Cassie replied with a clear sense of nervousness in her voice. "And, um, did you get a chance to talk to Pamela?"

Carl hated to follow his good news with such a let down, but he had to be honest with Cassie.

"Yes, actually, we had quite a good conversation, and I asked her quite directly to pray about a gift of a million dollars. I have to be honest with you. Her response was not promising. I know that she'll give a gift that she believes to be generous, probably the biggest gift she's ever given, but she made it clear it would not be anywhere near what we asked for. Now Cassie, we don't know what God may still do in her heart. But as your friend, I need to encourage you to begin looking at other alternatives if we're not able to raise all the money to buy the house. I'm sorry. I know this is a bit of a blow. We need to work hard and be faithful in trying to raise the money, but we also need to be realistic and think seriously about a plan B."

There was a long silence on the phone. With every second that passed, Carl's heart got heavier. It was so frustrating knowing that Pamela could easily write that check, but he had to leave that between her and God. All he could do was to be honest with Cassie and wait for her reply.

"Is she coming to the meeting?" Cassie finally responded

"Oh, yes, sorry I didn't mention that. Yes, she's very interested in coming to the meeting and hearing your story."

"Then all we can do is work our plan, pray hard, and watch what God will do. The problem is, Carl, I don't have a plan B other than moving out of this house and finding a new location. If it comes to that, then that's what we'll do, and I know God will provide us a new place. I'm confident of that. But I've just been at this spot too many times not to believe that somehow God will again provide."

Carl deeply admired her faith, but he could hear in her voice that this was stretching her to her very limit.

"Cassie, I know he will provide in one form or another. Send out those letters. We'll see you a week from Tuesday. If there is anything else I can do in the meantime, please don't hesitate to ask."

"Thanks, Carl. You've done so much. Now I need to run some errands and prepare for the meeting. In other words, I need to go pick up a whole bunch of dimes."

Cassie's Story

River Haven had done a nice job preparing for the evening event. Chairs were arranged in a semicircle, and a table was decorated in autumn orange and arrayed with the usual church fare: coffee, juice, and a nice assortment of baked goods. Cassie and her staff had arrived early to check on the preparations and have a time of prayer before the guests arrived.

Carl and Cheryl were on their way to pick up Pamela.

"This should be a very interesting evening," Cheryl said. "This could turn everything around for Pamela's life."

"And for Cassie's," Carl added. "I just hope she comes with an open heart and gives herself a chance to really think and pray about the need. I know that if she'll listen and really seek God's heart, she'll be led to give far more than she ever dreamed. Maybe even the million dollars. Who knows?"

Cheryl replied, "You don't sound very confident that she'll actually give the gift."

"I'll admit my faith is pretty shaky. I know God can do anything, but you should've seen Pamela's face when I mentioned it to her."

The two drove on quietly, each in prayer for the night ahead.

Tom arrived at the church a little early to make sure things were set up properly. At his side was Bernice, his bride of forty-seven years. They greeted Cassie and the staff and made them feel welcome. Tom had resigned himself to the fact that this might be a good thing, even though he knew there would be a number of River Haven members at the event. He was still convinced that their generosity tonight would only add to the deficit the church was facing. But he and Bernice also cared a great deal for Esther's

71

House, and so it was with mixed emotions that he straightened some of the chairs, checked the coffee, and began to greet the guests as they arrived.

Aaron and Connie were among the first to arrive. Aaron greeted Tom.

"Tom, the room looks great. I really appreciate the support you and the stewardship committee have given this event. Let's pray some hearts are changed."

Connie hugged Bernice and Tom, and then they found their way to Cassie and the staff. Aaron had a short time of prayer with them and then made his way to his seat.

As Tom stood in the back of the room greeting people, he couldn't help but feel his anxiety increase as member after member came and found a seat. There was something eating away at Tom, something he'd kept deep inside himself. Tonight it was boiling to the surface.

Carl and Cheryl arrived at Pamela's house, and Carl went to the door and found her in the entryway putting on her coat. "Ready to go?" Carl asked.

"Yes, thank you. It's a lovely night, and I hope there's a great turnout for this." As Pamela walked to the door that Carl was holding open, she stopped and looked at him and motioned to her purse. "I've done what you said and prayed about this. I have my gift with me to give to Cassie." With that she was out the door and down to the car to greet Cheryl and climb in.

Carl was greatly disappointed. He'd hoped she would wait until she heard Cassie's story before making her decision. He couldn't imagine that she would've made the kind of gift he was hoping for just based on their conversation a week ago. He fought off his discouragement, locked the door behind him, and headed for the car.

By 7:05, all the guests had arrived and were taking their seats. Jack and Rita Post sat in the second row, and Rebecca sat next to them. Across the aisle Jeannie and Bill sat next to Bernice, who was saving a seat for Tom. Peter showed up a little late and took a seat in the back. Carl, Cheryl, and Pamela arrived in time to find a good seat in the third row that was squarely in front of where Cassie would be sharing. The whole group numbered about forty-eight. Carl thanked God for the wonderful turnout and he smiled as Cassie and Tom came up front and focused the attention of the group.

"On behalf of the stewardship committee at River Haven," Tom started, "I am pleased to welcome you here this evening for this very special time and for this very important cause. We're all here because we care deeply about the ministry at Esther's House. We all received a letter from Cassie, and we know they are facing a significant challenge. But God is great, and so I want to thank you for joining us this evening to see what he can do among us. I'd like to turn this over to pastor Aaron, who will open us in prayer." With that, Tom sat next to Bernice, who patted his arm and gave him an approving smile.

Aaron also thanked the group and opened with a prayer, commending the entire evening into God's hands. Then he introduced Cassie.

Carl could never remember seeing Cassie in a dress and wearing makeup and jewelry. She looked great, and Carl knew it was an indication of how seriously she took the meeting. She was pulling out all the stops. She smiled and began.

"Thank you so much for being here. Just your presence at this meeting gives me such great encouragement. As I look across this room, I see the faces of so many people who have stood with us over the past years. You are the reason Esther's House continues to flourish and minister to dozens of young women every year. We are changing lives by the power of God and the name of Jesus, and so much of that is because of all of you."

Cassie went on to talk about the relationship that Esther's House had with the woman who owned it, about her passing, the letter from the attorney, and the ultimatum. Cassie pulled the attorney's letter out of her pocket and read it to the assembly of supporters. Heads shook slowly as they heard again the cost of the house and the deadline. Cassie finished the letter, folded it up, and put it back in her pocket. She then looked up at the group.

"I still shake when I read that letter. Today is November twenty-third, so we have seven days to respond. I want to thank my dear friend Carl Burns for helping me prepare for this evening and putting this event together. We really felt the best thing to do was to be honest and share our need with all of you and then pray to see what God might put on your hearts. But Carl asked me something else. He asked if I would share my story with all of you. I prayed a lot about that. It's not easy standing up in front of people you care about and sharing the pain and mistakes of your past. But along with those mistakes, there is a wonderful testimony to the goodness and faithfulness of God, and for that reason I agreed to share with you tonight. Please know that I don't want this to be about me. I want to glorify God, and I hope you hear that in what I share. I'm going to give you the *Reader's Digest* version, and I hope it won't take too long."

Comments from the group encouraged her to take all the time she needed. People settled back and got comfortable as Cassie took a big drink of water and a deep breath before beginning.

"I was raised in a pretty typical middle-class home. My mom was a schoolteacher, and my dad owned a security company. I have one older brother, Rick. As a family, we went to church on

Christmas and Easter and pretty much ignored it the rest of the year. I was just a normal kid. That all changed when I was nine years old and my mom died of a rare heart condition. It about killed my dad. It was the most challenging year of my life, or so I thought at the time. I didn't know at that point what all God had in store for me. The first amazing thing that God did in our lives was that, through the death of my mom, my dad became a deeply committed Christian. We began going to church regularly. His faith really helped him get through the loss of my mom. I had exactly the opposite reaction. I was angry with God because I suddenly had to live the rest of my life without the approval and support of a mother. I was close to my dad, but every time we went to church, all I saw were hypocrites. Just after I turned ten, one of my best friends was molested by one of the deacons in the church. She never reported it, but it just cemented in my mind how much I hated the church and the God they worshiped.

Cassie took a deep breath and continued. "Later that year I got drunk for the first time, and for next fourteen years my life was consumed by every kind of drug and alcohol abuse you can imagine. Scarcely a day went by when I didn't have some substance in my system. It was so hard on my dad, but he kept loving me and praying for me. He would talk to me about his faith, but I wanted nothing to do with it. I made a vow never to step foot in the front door of a church again. I even avoided weddings in order to keep that vow.

"When I was seventeen, I got pregnant. We got married, and that lasted for about six months before he left me. Three years later, I got married again and had a second child. You might have seen pictures of my kids on my desk. Nathan and Sophie are the loves of my life. I prided myself on raising normal children, even though my own life was falling apart.

"One night while I was out with friends, I tried methamphetamine for the first time. I only tried it because there was no cocaine available. As soon as it hit my system, I fell in love with the drug. From that point on, it was all I used, and it completely took over my life.

"Not long after Sophie was born, her dad and I got divorced. I became a single mom. I got a great job working as an office manager for a law firm. The ironic thing was, when I was at the law firm, I was not only high, but I began dealing meth as well. The money was great, and I needed it in order to save up to send my kids to college. So if you'd looked at us about twelve years ago, you would've seen a typical, middle-class, single-parent family. I had a respectable job, nice house, a new car, and two beautiful children who were doing well in school. But on the side, I was doing meth and building a business as a dealer with the Mexican mafia."

As she finished that sentence, she could hear the gasps of a number of people in the group. Everyone was on the edge of their seats trying to take in this information. Most of the supporters of Esther's House knew that Cassie had a tough background, but none of them were quite prepared for this. Carl prayed that people would be receptive and sympathetic, not judgmental. He gave Cassie a big smile of encouragement.

She continued. "Then one day my whole world came crashing down. Nathan and Sophie went to be with their grandfather for three weeks. While they were gone, I realized how much freedom I would have to get high and to deal if I didn't have the responsibility of the kids. Even though I loved them dearly, the meth had overtaken my life. I called Dad and told him I was moving out of the house and that he needed to take care of the kids for a while. I moved in with a friend. In the first few days I was there, he stole all my money and all of the meth I had to deal, and he disappeared. I knew I would never be able to explain what happened to my boss, and I was terrified. I knew my life was in danger, so I stuffed the few things I had with me in a bag and took off walking in order to clear my mind and think. A few hours later, I found myself in front of the Liberty Motel. It looked like a good place to hide out for while and try to rebuild my business. I went in to see if there was any way that I could get a room at least for one night, even though I didn't have any money. That's when God brought the first miracle into my life."

Cassie went on to tell the group the story about her time at the Lib, her friendship with Alastair Nicol, and her conversion. And then she told the story of that one-dollar bill and the first time she put a dime in her pocket and trusted God to always provide.

Many in the crowd wiped away tears in their eyes as they relived that moment with her. The whole group was visibly moved by Cassie's story. The air was thick with emotion, and there was not a sound as she continued.

"My friends, ever since that day I have kept this dime in my pocket. At first it was a reminder to me to commit the first ten percent of everything I had to God. But that was not the real reason God gave me this dime. It took me some time to learn the lesson he wanted for me, and the real reason I wanted to share my story with you tonight.

"I want to tell you about one more amazing thing that happened since coming clean and moving into Esther's House, and then I'll be done. It happened not long after I arrived there."

Cassie shared the story about giving the fifty-dollar bill to Walt in response to his message at that first capital campaign meeting.

"That was the scariest gift I've ever given. But in the next two weeks, I was offered a few part-time jobs that were just what I needed. Now I don't want to say that there's an automatic matcrial blessing that comes every time we give generously, but that whole episode taught me two lessons. The first is that you can't out-give God. I mean, you just can't be too generous, too faithful, too obedient. He really does meet our needs, even when he asks us to give more than we really think we can. That's happened in my life over and over again, and I'm really starting to believe it," she said with a smile and a laugh.

"The second lesson is that having God and God alone is enough. What God put on my heart that week was this thought: 'If all I had in life was God and a dime, that would be enough!' That's when the meaning of this dime in my pocket changed significantly. It wasn't about me giving ten percent of what I had. It was about me giving everything I had. God doesn't want ten percent. He wants all of me, and he had to get me to the point were I was willing to say and believe that all I need in life is God. He gave me this dime to remind me of that," she said as she pulled the dime from her pocket and held it up in front of her. She just stood there for a moment rolling it around in her fingers and thinking again what it represented to her. Then she put it back in her pocket and reached in her bag and pulled out a roll of dimes. She broke open the paper wrapping and began walking around the room, handing a dime to each person.

"This is my gift to you this evening. I know you came here thinking that I needed something from you, but I've come to learn that all of life is about giving, not receiving. I want you to have a dime to remind you of these two lessons."

Tom and Jack jumped up and helped her distribute the dimes to everyone. It was amazing to watch a roomful of affluent people give so much attention to a single dime. Each person looked at it, really looked at it, and considered Cassie's words. No one put theirs away; they each just held it in their hands or between their fingers or in an open palm. Once everyone had a dime, Cassie continued.

"It's my prayer that this dime will be a constant reminder that God owns everything and that he is always faithful. My question to you tonight is this: If all you were left with in life was this dime and God, would that be enough?" And with that Cassie sat down.

Carl and Cassie had agreed that he would say some closing words when she was done. He sat there for several moments allowing Cassie's words to sink in. Then he stood up and addressed the group.

"I really don't know how to follow that incredible story. I just have a few things to say, and then we will end for the evening. I've known Cassie for about four years, and I have never heard her whole story. I know there's a lot more she could tell, but I just want to say thank you, Cassie, for being so open with all of us this evening. I'm going to have to think long and hard about how I would answer that question, 'Is God and a dime enough?' I just want to say a couple words about logistics. You all were sent a response card for you to use to indicate what God has put on your heart to help the ministry buy this house. If you're able to make that decision tonight and leave the form with us, then please hand it to Cassie or me. If you need more time to think and pray, that's fine, but we would ask you to return them to us by the twenty-eighth so that we know where we stand and can be ready to reply to the attorney. I guess I just want to close by saying that there are no shortages of resources in the kingdom of God. If he wants Cassie to buy that home, then he has the resources in your pockets and mine to make that happen. It's just really a question about our obedience. Thank you again for coming. At this time, I would like to ask a very special friend if he would come up and close us with a blessing."

Everyone looked around for a moment to see who the mystery guest might be. Then from the back, a man stood up and walked to the front with a huge grin on his face.

"Alastair!" Cassie shrieked, running to him and giving him a huge hug. People applauded and stood as the two shared a few quick words of greeting. Then the tall Scotsman turned to the group and got their attention.

"I'd just like to say 'amen' to everything Cassie shared with you tonight. I hope you'll all pray about this need. We need Esther's House. This community and this city need Esther's House. And I know there is someone that God is calling to step forward in faith and help Cassie buy that house. Now please join hands and let's close this wonderful night with the Lord's Prayer."

Carl held Pamela's hand on one side and Cheryl's on the other. Cheryl squeezed his hand so tight he thought his knuckles would crack. As the words of the Lord's Prayer leapt from his lips, he added his own prayer. "Lord, let Pamela have ears to hear and a heart to respond. I pray she is your instrument for this gift."

Immediately after the "amen," a number of Cassie's supporters went to her and hugged her and Alastair and told her how deeply moved they were by her story. You could see by the look on everyone's faces that Cassie's testimony had impacted them deeply. Carl returned to his seat and tried to read Pamela's face. He expected her to take her pledge form out of her purse, hand it to Cassie, and that would be that. Instead, Pamela rose and walked over to the coat rack and retrieved her overcoat. Carl followed her a bit confused.

"Pamela, would you like me to take you home now?" Carl asked.

"Yes, I need to think about some things, and I'd like to do that at home," she replied, showing little emotion in her voice. Carl found Cheryl, and after a quick word of thanks to Tom and Aaron, he escorted them out to the car.

Cassie spent more than an hour talking with people, thanking them for coming, and receiving response forms from about half of those who attended. By 9:30, she was exhausted. She thanked Tom and Aaron one more time, gave Alastair a huge hug, and left with two of her staff members.

After Aaron had sent Connie home, he slipped up into his office for some quiet time. Cassie's story had impacted him deeply. He sat behind his desk and looked around at all of the trappings of his profession: his library of scholarly books, his diplomas, pictures of his graduation and installation, his file cabinets full of sermons and bible studies he had given over the years. Then he looked down at his dime and considered how it seemed that he depended upon everything but God alone. He depended on his own skills for his preaching, on the stewardship committee to be sure they had the money they needed, on his staff and volunteers to run the programs—the list went on. He realized that while River Haven did a great job worshiping God, they never really had to trust him. They had things pretty well figured out for themselves.

He was rolling his dime around in his hand and considering what all this might mean to his ministry when Tom knocked quietly on the door and looked in.

"Do you need to be alone, Pastor, or do you mind if I join you?" he asked.

"No, no, come in and join me. I could use some words of wisdom," he replied with a smile.

"None here, just a heart that's churning around a bit." Tom sat down across the desk from Aaron. "So, what has all this put on your mind, if you don't mind my asking," Tom inquired.

Aaron thought for a moment about how he could put all this into words. He was grateful Tom was there. He needed to try to sort this out.

"Between what Carl shared with us and Cassie's story tonight, I guess I feel like it's the whole question of whether or not we really live our lives in ways that require us to trust in God. I mean, Cassie's question is a great challenge, but how many of us ever really get to be in the position where we *have* to trust in God because that's all we have? I'm not sure you can answer the question until he gets you to that ultimate point of total need. And I don't want to get there! So how do we develop an absolute trust in God to provide all of our needs when we spend so much of our time providing for our own needs? And when we really are never in need?" he asked.

Tom and Aaron just sat quietly for a few moments as the words hung in the air. Then Tom replied, "I guess it's that journey Carl talks about. It's not about ever reaching the destination but always letting God move us in that direction. Don't beat yourself up, Pastor. You're battling the world, the values we see all around us, and lots of love of money. It's a big challenge, and I don't think we've been very helpful to you as a stewardship committee."

"I think that's just it, Tom. I'm not *battling* the world. I'm not in the battle at all," Aaron said, sitting up and leaning across his desk. "I'm so concerned about what people think that I'm paralyzed by the thought of challenging them. I care more what my congregation wants of me than what God called me here to do. I guess I'm realizing that you can't be a people pleaser and a faithful minister at the same time. The two just can't be held together."

"Well, you're right about one thing. This congregation won't be too pleased with a lot of focus on stewardship. I know pastors who have lost their jobs when they tried to push that talk too far," Tom replied.

Aaron nodded and replied, "So what it comes down to is whether I see myself as an owner of my church or a steward. I remember that line distinctly in what Carl shared a few weeks ago. I guess my biggest confession is that I have been an owner. This is *my* church. These are *my* members. I've held on so tightly to that. Now I need to figure out a way to give it all back to God and embrace my role as a steward." He looked up at Tom and added, "Any ideas on where I should start?"

Tom stood up and went over to Aaron's bookcase. He reached up and pulled down the finance committee report binder, brought it back over, and sat it down in front of Aaron. Aaron was completely surprised. He gave Tom an inquisitive look.

"What's this all about?" He asked.

Tom sat down and leaned forward with his elbows on his knees. He rubbed his hands together, looking down at them for a moment, and then looked up at his pastor.

"I have something to tell you, Pastor, and it has a lot to do with what you've just been talking about and what's in the back of that little binder. I know you've never looked back there to see what people give. Well, I have. I think Kevin and I are the only two people in the church who have. He's the head of your finance committee, and I'm the head of your stewardship committee, and we're the only two that know what people give in this congregation. If you looked at it, I think you'd find a few things that would shock you. So here's one of them. Bernice and I are the biggest givers here at River Haven. By a long shot. For a long time, it didn't bother me because I just felt we needed to give what God led us to give. But over the years, I've grown bitter over the fact that our giving is so much more than anyone else in the congregation, and there are some pretty well off people here. I'm going to tell you something, Pastor, not to blow my own horn but to try to make a point. For the last four years, Bernice and I wrote a check at the end of the year to balance the budget. A couple of years, it was a pretty darn big check. Each year I got more and more angry that other people weren't giving what they should. All the happiness I used to have in giving to the church went away. Well, last year it bothered me so much that I told Bernice that we were going to cut back our giving as well. She was madder than ... well, let's just say she didn't agree. But I insisted, and my stubbornness won the day. So for most of this year, we have given about half of what we used to. Pastor, that's the biggest reason were in such a deficit. I wanted to force this crisis to see if people would finally step up to the plate. I got my wish, but after tonight, I'm realizing just how foolish I've been. Damned old fool, actually."

Aaron was stunned. He knew that Tom and Bernice had done well in their wheat land farming in eastern Washington before moving to Seattle, but there were no signs that they were this wealthy. Tom continued.

"So, I guess one point I want to make is this: If you had been reading these numbers in the back of this report, you would've seen how our giving had dropped off this year. I think you would've come to me and asked me what was going on, and when I told you, you probably would've challenged me on what I was thinking. I think I needed you to know, because I needed you to minister to me. I was really hurting—still am. But you would never know that because you've never looked in the back of that binder. I think it's time to start doing so, if you don't mind my saying, Pastor."

Aaron picked up the binder and looked up at Tom. "Well, Tom, I think you're right. I want to apologize for not being there when you needed me. I've avoided this because I was afraid of offending people. I was afraid of what I might think of people if I knew what they gave. I approached this whole thing as an owner, holding on to my old, worldly ways of thinking about money. I think it's time for me to set aside my desire to own my church and to be liked in everything I do. How did Carl put it? To step off the throne of my little kingdom I call First Church of River Haven and begin really being a pastor to this congregation." He pondered that thought for a moment, and then remembered Tom's comments.

"And I want to thank you and Bernice for all you've done. I could've done this year's ago, but the important thing is I'm doing it now. I think I understand a little better why you've taken the role on the stewardship committee. Yes, a lot of things make sense now. Tom, I'm going to need your help. This is a huge step in a new direction for this congregation, and we need leaders like you to help us along on this journey."

"I'll do whatever I can. I still think we need to send out a letter, but it needs to say more of what Carl suggested. And Pastor, Bernice and I will take care of the deficit again this year. But this time, I'm going do it happily."

There was very little conversation on the short drive from the church back to Pamela's house. Carl could feel the tension in Pamela's presence, and he didn't know how to read it. Pamela sat in the back seat and was staring out the window. Cheryl quietly reached over and squeezed Carl's arm as he drove. Neither of them knew what to expect next. Carl drove up the circular drive and stopped just outside the large, white double front doors.

"Please come in. This will just take me a few minutes," Pamela said. They both walked with her into the entry. "If you can just wait in the kitchen, I'll be done soon."

Pamela walked into her office and pulled the two glass French doors closed behind her. Carl and Cheryl went across the hall into the kitchen.

Looking back across the hall and through the glass panes of the study's French doors, they could see Pamela studying some documents that lay on the desk in front of her. After several minutes, they could see her prepare an envelope, and then she shut off her lamp and walked to the study doors.

"Do you think it could be?" Cheryl asked quietly.

Carl nodded. "Yes, I really think it could be."

Pamela came out of her study and handed an envelope to Carl.

"Can you take this to Cassie? I'm pretty tired, and I would like to turn in. Thank you for taking me and … well, for everything," she said, handing the envelope to Carl.

"I don't know what to say, Pamela. But thank you. I'm sure you'll hear from Cassie in the morning." Carl and Cheryl gave her a hug and were out the door.

As they walked to the car, Cheryl couldn't contain her emotions. "I am going to die a thousand deaths before we get that envelope to Cassie," she burst out. "Do you think she'll still be up at the house?"

"I think so, and I'm sure going to go by and get her up if she's not. I'm as excited as you are," Carl replied.

They drove to Esther's House, and when they arrived they saw lights on inside. They parked in front and almost ran up to the front door. Carl rang the doorbell, knowing he may be waking up some of the staff, but on this night, with this envelope in his pocket, he didn't care.

Cassie answered the door and was surprised to see Carl and Cheryl standing there smiling like a couple of Cheshire cats.

"Hi, wow, it's nice to see you, but what…?" she stammered. Carl just held up the envelope and smiled.

"I have something for you from Pamela. May we come in?" he asked teasingly.

Cassie hurried them into the living room. She took the envelope and just looked at it.

"I can hardly bring myself to open it, Carl. My hands are shaking."

Cassie sighed deeply and settled herself. Carl and Cheryl held hands as they watched Cassie carefully work open the envelope. She pulled the check out and opened it. Instead of looking at it, she looked up to the ceiling for a moment. When she let her eyes fall down on the check, Carl and Cheryl stared at her face to catch the emotion as she saw the figure. They immediately knew that something was wrong. Cassie put her hand to her mouth and fought back some tears that began rolling down her cheeks. She looked up to her two friends and said quietly, "It's a very nice gift, very generous." Then she handed it to Carl.

He turned it around and focused his eyes on the number, which had been neatly and carefully written out by Pamela. Cheryl was pressed up against him to read it for herself. Together they saw it: $10,000. Carl looked again to be sure he saw all of the decimal points. But there was no mistaking it. He read the longhand version and it confirmed, "ten thousand dollars."

Cassie said again, "It is a very generous gift, a lot more than she has ever given. Will you thank her for me?" Carl thought of doing a lot of things, but thanking her was not among them.

Cheryl slumped back in her seat and said quietly, "I can't believe it." She looked up at Cassie, who was trying to put on a brave front.

"Cassie, I'm sorry. We all really thought ... I mean ... I just really expected that after tonight she would ... " Cheryl didn't know how to even finish the sentence.

Carl handed the check back to Cassie. "I will let her know that you appreciate her generosity. Cassie, I'm truly sorry. This was a great evening. You did a wonderful job. We did all we could. Let's sleep on this and come back tomorrow when we are more rested."

Cassie got up and looked out the window into the dark street. "I don't think tomorrow will bring anything new. I've looked at the response forms we received, and they are all very generous, but not anywhere near enough to buy this house. When we come back from Thanksgiving, I'll call the attorney. Then we'll start looking for another home."

Retreat from the Edge of Freedom

A SINGLE LIGHT SHONE above the sink in Pamela's kitchen as she poured herself a glass of water and took her evening pills. She put away a few remaining dishes and turned to leave the kitchen. As she looked through the French doors into her study across the hall, she paused for a moment, then gave in to the impulse to go back into her office. She turned on her brass desk lamp and sat down in her chair behind her desk. She didn't know why, but she had to look at it one more time. She opened a small letter drawer on the left side of her desk and took out the envelope that still bore the crease where she had folded it and put it in her purse earlier that evening. Underneath the envelope was a check. She took it from the drawer and held it under the lamp to examine it. She sighed deeply as she read the name she had neatly printed on it: Esther's House Campaign. Then she looked again at the amount: One Million Dollars. She thought back to the events of the past three days, including the moment when she had written those words with such conviction.

AFTER HER VISIT WITH Carl, Pamela could not get his words out of her mind. For several evenings, she sat looking at photographs of the happy years she had spent with Stephen. He was always laughing and helping all those around him do the same. Stephen lived life with a light heart. Pamela missed him so deeply that she ached physically every time the emptiness of the house or a flicker of a memory forced upon her the cold reality that she would never see him again. How she wanted his joyful spirit and deep faith to guide her in this important decision.

"Would you really have me give this gift if you were here?" she asked quietly as she ran her fingers across her favorite photo of the two of them on an anniversary trip to the Grand Canyon. In her spirit, she knew the answer was yes. For the next several days, Pamela did something she had not done in years, she opened her Bible and began reading and praying for God's guidance. In that rich fellowship, Pamela's heart began to soften. She recalled several of the verses that Carl had shared with her. They spoke to her in a powerful way.

Three days before the meeting at River Haven, Pamela sat at her desk after an especially moving time in the scriptures and prepared to make the decision on what she would give to Esther's House. She could scarcely believe that she was about to write this kind of check. She looked over at the large table with all of the financial reports still assembled in their neat stacks. She had read over them in the previous days, and although her anxiety over her finances had only ebbed slightly, she sensed a newfound freedom in her spirit. She had wrestled with her finances for so long she hardly remembered what it was like to be free from that anxiety. But now the Spirit was beginning to work in her heart, and she experienced a level of peace she had thought would never be hers again. As she sat at her desk, that peace transformed her attitude regarding the gift she was about to give.

"Well, Lord, if this is the journey Carl has been talking about, I guess this is a very big first step," she said in a quiet prayer as she penned "Esther's House Campaign" on the check and then the numerals "$1,000,000." Pamela expected to be jarred back to her senses once she really looked at what she had written. But all she felt was quietness in her heart and a deep sense of satisfaction in knowing what this gift would mean to Cassie. She put the check in the letter drawer of her desk and left her study with a lighter heart than she had known since Stephen passed away.

The day of the Esther's House gathering, however, all of that changed. It began with a morning call from her broker. He shared the news that a major investment of hers would take much longer to pay then they had expected. At noon, she sat and watched a news show in which a leading economists predicted a significant downturn in the economy. She felt her heart race as the stock market fell in response. All of the old fears now came flooding back into her mind. She sat for hours poring over financial statements and calling her broker for reassurances that her estate would remain intact. By late in the afternoon her fear had driven her back to her desk, where she sat trembling, holding the check that just the day before seemed to be the symbol of a newfound freedom and a long overdue joy.

"What was I thinking," she muttered to herself. She placed the check in the letter drawer of her desk and pulled out her check register. She again printed the name of Esther's House Campaign on a new check. Her hand was shaking as the pen sat poised above the next line. She dared not pray for fear of what her heart might tell her. With clenched teeth she wrote the figure "$10,000." She tore the check from her book, not allowing herself a moment to think about what she had done. She placed it in the envelope, folded in half, and put it in her purse.

Four hours later, she was sitting in the little gathering at the River Haven Church listening to a young woman challenging her to give in a way that would help her find that place of joy in obedience to a God who always provides. Pamela was completely undone. With a ten-thousand dollar check in her purse and a one-million dollar check in her desk drawer, her heart was torn. Her conscience was too deeply troubled to make a decision on the spot. She asked Carl and Cheryl to drive her back to her house, where she could think and pray through this important decision one more time.

As the two of them stood in the kitchen watching her through her glass study doors, Pamela again reached inside her desk and pulled out the million-dollar check. She sat with the two checks side by side on her desk. One represented her fear and the other her freedom. She took one more moment to pray, to think, and to decide. In that moment, with the two checks in front of her, Pamela knew in her spirit what she should do, but she simply couldn't do it. She could not break free from eight years of self-reliance, eight years of trusting in her own intuition, eight years of holding on tightly to what she had, eight years of watching every penny, agonizing over every investment decision, and studying every financial move. They had produced in her spirit a sense of absolute ownership. Now, as she looked on the two checks, she was living securely behind the reinforced concrete walls that she had built around her own little kingdom Even with the voice of her husband ringing in her ears, even with the movement of the Spirit stirring deeply inside her soul, Pamela set aside her chance at freedom and retreated back into the walls of her lonely sanctuary. She took the million-dollar check and placed it back in the letter drawer of her desk, inserted the ten-thousand dollar check into the envelope, and left her study to give it to Carl and Cheryl.

Now she was back staring at that same check. The decision had been made, the deed had been done. Pamela felt no remorse, nor did she feel the slightest bit of happiness. She just felt empty. A steely determination welled up in her spirit. She held the check between her fingers and tore it in half.

"I must've been insane," she said quietly to herself. She placed the two halves into the shredder at the side of her desk, and as the high-pitched screech of the shredding blades did their work, she shut out her light, left her study, and went to bed.

Jehovah Jireh

THANKSGIVING CAME AND WENT. Carl and Cheryl had a house full of family and friends, including Pamela. Carl had called her the day before to thank her for the gift to Esther's House. He decided to be positive, and he mustered all the conviction he could to be sure his tone did not betray his true emotions. Nothing more was said of it at Thanksgiving, and the day passed with all the focus on food and family and gratitude.

River Haven had a service of thanksgiving and praise and Aaron chose some new words to describe what it meant to give thanks to a God who is so very faithful in all things. Perhaps only a few in the congregation picked up on it, but it was Aaron's first step in his new role as chief steward of his flock.

At Esther's House, the staff put on a full Thanksgiving spread for the women at the house, and several family members and friends were there as well. The table seated twenty-four, and every seat was occupied. Cassie was her usual bubbly self, which hid her deep distress at what the following week would require of her and everyone at the ministry.

The following days passed slowly until November 29 arrived. Cassie had watched the mail for the remaining response forms. When the last one arrived, she knew for certain that the house was lost. Together they totaled the anticipated two hundred thousand dollars. She would ask the attorney if they would accept it as a down payment and carry the rest, but she already knew the answer. He had let her know that several interested buyers had already approached the daughter. There was no room for negotiation. Carl called to check in on her and offer any last minute help he could provide, but she assured him she was fine and had resigned herself to the inevitable. "I know God has a great new place for us, so I need to be strong and focus on his future for the ministry."

Late November had offered up an unusually warm and sunny day, so after breakfast, Cassie used the opportunity to walk around the large yard and garden that was laid to rest for the wet winter. She strolled around the grounds just to absorb in her soul the feeling of the place. Several times she broke down at the thought of never enjoying another spring here. She would miss the honeysuckle that filled the air with perfume every May. She had planted over fifty new daffodil bulbs that someone else's eyes would enjoy. Every turn brought back memories of conversations, prayers, and lives of young women being changed forever. "The ministry will go on. It's bigger than just a house and a garden," she said to herself.

One last time she reached down to press her fingers against the dime in her pocket and said again, "He will provide. He always has." She couldn't put it off any longer. She stopped to take one more look around, and as she turned to make her way back to the house to make the call, she heard a shout from the direction of the back door.

"Cass, someone's here to see you," the voice rang out.

Cassie took one last look at the garden she so loved and made her way back to the house. She noticed a car parked out in front, but she didn't recognize it. As she entered the house, she was surprised to see Tom and Bernice waiting for her.

"Tom, Bernice, it's nice to see you. Thanks for stopping by," she said with a voice betraying her curiosity.

They walked into the kitchen, and Tom accepted an offer for a cup of coffee. Bernice looked at the quilts that had been made by the residents as part of their occupational therapy.

"These are just beautiful, Cassie. You've done so much for these women," she said warmly. "Tom and I have been so pleased to be able to support you and your work. It really brings joy to our hearts to see what you are doing here."

Cassie remembered their granddaughter's story. "I haven't asked in a long time, but how is Amanda?"

"Doing much better, thanks," Tom replied. "She's finally kicked her addiction to meth, but she has a long ways to go to get her life back together."

Bernice added, "Cassie, we were so moved by your own story. It gave us hope that Amanda will find her way as well. Thank you again for being such a friend to help us through those difficult days." She took Cassie's hand and patted it, giving her a look of true thankfulness. Cassie was humbled by their words and appreciated their friendship, but she sensed there was something below the surface in their visit.

"So, how did the fundraiser turn out?" Tom asked. It was at that moment that Cassie realized that she never received a response from Tom and Bernice. She realized that they must have come by to make their gift, which was a nice gesture, she thought.

"Everyone was very generous, but I'm afraid we are well short of our goal," she replied. She had hoped for five thousand from them, maybe ten thousand, but that was all a moot point now. She would be gracious in response to whatever they had come to give.

"So how far are we?" Tom asked.

"I'm sorry?" she replied, not sure what he meant.

"How far are we from the goal to buy the house?" he explained.

"Oh, well, we are about one million dollars short. Quite a ways, I'm afraid. I'm planning on calling the attorney this morning, and tomorrow we will start looking for a new place to call Esther's

House. It's tough, but I know God will provide for us," she said as courageously as she could.

"Well, Bernice and I haven't made our pledge yet. We've been talking a lot this week about thanksgiving, life, priorities, ownership, two-kingdoms and about trust, generosity, and joy. And all the while, we've been playing with these little dimes someone gave us," he said with a twinkle in his eye.

Cassie smiled back at him and enjoyed his wit, but she was focused on the call she needed to make and was anxious to get it over with. She hoped Tom would get to the point quickly.

"Cassie, we're sorry to have waited so long to make our gift. We really needed to think and pray about it," Bernice said. Then she came up to Cassie and took hold of both of her hands. She stood looking directly into her eyes, which totally surprised Cassie. Tom moved up behind Bernice and put his huge hand on her shoulder. He had a big grin on his face.

Bernice spoke slowly. "Cassie, you said that if you were faithful, God would always provide. Now we know that there was someone you were counting on to give you the money you needed to buy this house. And we know you didn't get it. You needed someone in your life that would step forward and be used by God to, well, bring you a miracle. In our life together, we have found that God is always faithful, but seldom in the way we expected. You see, Cassie, God did move in someone's heart to give you the money you need to buy this house, and it was us."

Cassie tensed up for a moment. She looked at Bernice, and then at Tom with total disbelief. She knew their hearts were in the right place, but they didn't have that kind of money.

Tom continued where Bernice left off. "We went back to our little town of Harvest for Thanksgiving, and I was sitting with my old friend Sam Roberts, telling him about the event at River

Haven and Esther's House and the money you needed. I told him we wanted to help, but that was a lot of money. Old Sam pointed across the wheat fields that our house looks out over and he asked me, 'Tom, how much of this land do you own?' I said, 'Well, about as far as you can see, over twenty thousand acres, maybe a little more.' Then he spun around and glared at me like only a friend can. He said, 'No, Tom, let me ask you again. How much land do *you* own?' Well, I got was he was getting at. Sam is one of the most generous people I know. He runs the little gospel mission in Harvest, and he taught me just about everything I know about giving to the Lord. So I apologized for being such a stupid old coot and replied, 'Okay, Sam, I don't own *any* of it. It all belongs to God.' So then Sam turns back to me and says, 'And how much of God's land do you think it would take to raise a million bucks?' And I said, 'Well, hell…'"

Bernice jabbed Tom in the side. "Tom, watch your language!"

"Sorry, I mean, well, heck, it wouldn't take a lot, I guess. That's what I said to Sam. He looked at me and said, 'So God has all this land just sitting here, a lot more than a million dollars worth, and this little gal in Seattle is going to lose her house because she doesn't have the money?' Well, that was all he had to say."

Bernice added, "I was standing in the doorway and heard the whole thing. I said, 'Praise the Lord.' I wanted to give the money to you last week. I mean for heaven's sake, we don't even need to sell any land to do that."

Cassie started shaking, and she turned a little pale.

"Dear, are you all right?" Bernice asked.

"I think I need to sit down," Cassie replied, and they led her to a chair at the kitchen table. She looked up at the smiling couple and asked, "Bernice, Tom, is this for real? I mean, I'm not doubting you, but are you saying what I think you're saying?"

Tom replied, "Cassie, it would be our privilege to make a gift of one million dollars so you can buy this house. We'd have brought a check, but that's a lot for any bank to accept, so we'll just transfer the funds into your account tomorrow if that's all right with you."

The next several minutes were a total blur. Hugs, tears, and cries of joy filled the Esther's House kitchen. Staff members came in to hear the news, but Tom and Bernice slipped away quietly and asked that their giving be kept anonymous. Before they left, Tom took Cassie's hand and said to her, "You keep up the good work here, and keep handing out those dimes. The one you gave me changed my life."

Two hours later, Cassie made her call to the attorney, then calls went out to Carl and Cheryl and a long list of the faithful supporters of Esther's House.

Remembering

CARL NAVIGATED HIS PRIUS through an unusual early November snowfall that was turning the streets icy. As he inched along, he passed by Esther's House and waved at one of the residents who was starting to clear away the snow from the front walk. It was about two weeks before Thanksgiving, almost a year after that tumultuous and amazing November. A lot had happened since the gathering at River Haven and the day Cassie received the miraculous gift.

Tom and Bernice had transferred the funds as promised, and six weeks later Cassie paid the full amount for the house in cash and received the signed deed to the old manor. Since then the ministry had flourished, but not without the need for continual maintenance to keep the home operating. Every time there was a need, someone in the community stepped up to meet it, and it was almost always a surprise. Cassie and the staff had come to expect it, although it challenged their faith every time.

The transformation in Aaron's life was remarkable. In January, he started preaching a series of sermons on Luke 12:15: "Then Jesus said to them, 'Watch out! Be on your guard against all kinds of greed; life does not consist in an abundance of possessions.'" As expected, he received a strong response. But his consistent message of God's abundance, our call to joyful and obedient generosity, and the Spirit's work of cultivating hearts that are rich toward God, slowly won over the majority of the congregation. Some members left, but those that remained began their own journeys toward becoming faithful stewards. It was not a smooth ride for the congregation. The year was filled with ups and downs, including a fire that damaged the kitchen and part of the auditorium.

But with every challenge, the congregation grew stronger. By September, Aaron felt they had matured enough to begin a discussion of what it means to be warriors in the battle for lordship. He would preach on becoming well-equipped stewards who live for Christ in a world that bows down to money and the control it brings.

He'd had coffee with Carl just before Labor Day and confessed that, despite the progress the congregation had made, he was still anxious about this upcoming series.

"We've talked about the two kingdoms, about stepping off our thrones and becoming one-kingdom people. We've talked about faithfulness and joy and generosity. But I've never laid it out as a real spiritual battle. I hope they're ready for it," he said. Over the next eight weeks, the Holy Spirit moved through the congregation and used Aaron's words to call a once docile, comfortable, and relatively apathetic congregation into engagement with their culture on a level no one ever thought possible. The First Church of River Haven was slowly becoming a formidable presence for the gospel in the city of Seattle.

Carl and Cheryl had continued on their own journey, and they were amazed at how many ways they found the old desire to rule over their own kingdoms was still present in their lives. Day by day and prayer-by-prayer, they continued to peel the onion and give more of themselves back to Christ. It would be a journey that would take them the rest of their lives, but their encounter with Cassie's story and the miracle gift from Tom and Bernice had motivated them to deeper levels of submission and commitment to Christ. However, Pamela's gift had also taught them an important lesson. In the weeks following the miracle gift, Cheryl, Carl, and Cassie had talked through in detail the events of that incredible November. In the midst of the joy and the wonder of God's amazing faithfulness. they were challenged by how much they still depended on their own logic and reason to bolster their faith. As long as they knew that Pamela had the resources to make the gift that was needed, they believed God would provide. But when that gift was lost, so was their faith. They all confessed to each other that through this experience God had taught them a profoundly important lesson. God's provision does not rely on our own ability to see how or when or by whom it may come. More often than not, God's provision will come from an unexpected place that defies our logic and is beyond our comprehension. Tom and Bernice had proven that, yet again, God will provide in his way according to his time, and it will always be more than enough and no sooner than we need it.

Tom and Bernice continued to enjoy life with their grandkids. Only a handful of people ever knew that they had been the ones who gave the gift that saved Esther's House. As the giving at River Haven increased through Aaron's leadership, the need for their significant giving decreased sharply. Yet they were giving more now than they ever had, and with a renewed sense of gratitude and joy. Tom still chaired the stewardship committee, but it had seven new members and a completely different focus. Meetings were spent primarily in prayer. The committee's new mission statement had just three words: Pray, Challenge, Model.

Carl had made it to the familiar turn that brought him to the driveway leading up to Pamela's house. It was his annual visit to discuss her finances and her giving. Pamela had been delighted at the news of the large gift that saved Esther's House, although she couldn't figure out who in that room had that kind of money. "Someone must've won the lottery," she replied. Sadly, throughout the year that followed, Carl had watched Pamela become more gripped by her anxiety over money. She would call him almost weekly to ask for advice on investments and seeking some sense of assurance that her plan would be adequate to meet her needs. Carl watched helplessly as the increase in the value of her estate was matched by her growing fear of losing it all. Month-by-month, Pamela began to age in both her appearance and her spirit. She went out less and pulled back from several relationships that had been important to her in the past. She was becoming a recluse.

It broke Carl's heart to see the effect her bondage to her finances was having on her entire life. Once again he would challenge her in her thinking, and once again she would thank him, promise to pray about it, and then retreat back into her sad, isolated life.

It all could have turned on one act of real generosity, Carl thought as he drove up the drive. *What a contrast between the newfound freedom being experienced by the members of River Haven and the deepening bondage that had seized Pamela's heart.*

As for Cassie, she was always looking for opportunities to share the story of what God had done in her life. On this particular day, not long after Carl had driven by, Cassie was busy working at Esther's House, getting ready for the morning women's Bible study. The house was full of women in recovery, and their resources were stretched to the limit. Soon they would need to think about additional staff members and possibly opening a second location to provide more space for the seemingly endless flow of young women desperately needing the safety and transforming power that they found in the rooms and corridors and loving hearts at Esther's House.

As she was putting away the final dishes from breakfast, there was a knock at the door. A middle-aged businessman greeted her when she went to answer it.

"Good morning. I hope I'm not bothering you. My name is Alex Grant. I just bought the real estate office down on the corner. I'm new in the area, and I just wanted to get acquainted with my neighbors. This is such a beautiful old house, and I see that you run some kind of organization out of it. Anyway, I don't want to take up any of your time, but I just thought I'd come by and say hello and find out more about what you do."

Cassie thanked him and invited him into the house. She gave him a quick overview of the work they do. She could tell by his response that he was not a believer. She prayed for an open door.

He looked around the large living room and out the windows to the sweeping lawn and asked, "So do you own this place?"

"No," she said. Then she walked over to her purse, reached inside, and pulled something out. She walked back over to Alex and invited him to sit down. She surprised him by asking for his hand, and when he offered it, she pressed a single dime into his palm. Then she looked up at him and smiled and said, "But if you have few minutes, I'd like to introduce you to the owner ... "

Perhaps the most telling indicator of what had happened in the lives of each of these people over the past year was what they chose to do with the dimes that Cassie had given them on that November evening.

Aaron had taken his dime, had it laminated, and secured it on the pulpit where he could see it each time he preached. It was a reminder to him of his commitment to be a steward of his congregation and to lead them on their mutual journey in cultivating hearts that were rich toward God.

Carl and Cheryl had taped theirs carefully to their bedroom bureau mirror. It would be the first thing they would look at when they got up in the morning and the last thing they would see before they went to bed at night. It was a reminder to them of their commitment to continue to offer every part of their lives back to God.

Carl had asked Pamela what she did with her dime. She couldn't remember.

Bernice had used her skill in cross-stitch to create a piece of embroidery into which she and Tom had fixed one of their dimes. They put it in a simple frame and hung it on the wall of their kitchen. Every morning, Tom and Bernice sat and read scripture together and prayed, and the presence of that framed cross-stitch was a constant reminder to them of the abundance of God's faithfulness and the joy of giving.

Bernice wanted the coin to be a testimony to their children and grandchildren of the power of a simple act of faith. So, after careful thought and prayer, and the approval of Tom, she embroidered four simple words in deep crimson across the top of the delicate frame: The Million-Dollar Dime.

A Word to My Brothers and Sisters in Christ

I wrote this story about Cassie, Carl, Aaron, Pamela, Tom, and Bernice as my way of sharing with you the amazing life that God has for all of us. We are all on a journey of becoming one-kingdom followers of Jesus Christ. It is the greatest journey of our lives! I pray this story has given you a glimpse of how different people at different stages of life engage in that journey.

I am convinced that God's highest purpose for our lives is that we cultivate hearts that are rich toward him. Our Creator God is an abundant giver, and we were created in his image to bear his likeness in the world. How else can we do that than by being lavish, generous givers ourselves?

My prayer is that you take away from this little story Cassie's two truths: *God owns it all and God will always provide*. If we let those two truths seep deep into our spirit, they will shed a light on all of the wrong attitudes and deeply ingrained habits that keep us from knowing the true joy of the faithful steward.

Those two truths are like handrails on a narrow path. Knowing that God owns it all keeps us from becoming owners ourselves. And knowing that God will always provide gives us the freedom to live in this world in a countercultural way, not seduced by all of the stuff that the world tells us we need in order to find happiness.

Hold on to those two rails. In between them is a path upon which God can work miracles in our hearts and transform us into agents of blessing. There is peace on that path. There is contentment on that path. There is the abundant life that Christ came to secure for all us on that path. It is the path of surrender, the path of unequivocal commitment, and the path of joy. On that path we lose our lives, and on that path we find them. On that path we abide in Christ, find our true identities, love our neighbors, and care for God's beautiful creation. On that path, God and God alone is all we need.

So let me end by asking you Cassie's question: "If all you had in life was God and a single dime, would that be enough?"

Welcome to the journey!

About the Author

DR. SCOTT RODIN IS a writer and international speaker on:
- Leadership as a Faithful Steward
- Raising Money as Kingdom Ministry
- The Journey of the Faithful Steward
- Three-Dimensional Discipleship
- Strategic Planning on Kingdom Values
- Creation Care

He has been serving not-for-profit organizations for the past twenty-eight years. He has served as counsel in fundraising, leadership development, and strategic planning to over one hundred organizations in the United States, Canada, Middle East, Great Britain, and Australia.

He is a Partner and Head of Strategic Alliances with Artios Partners, a training and resourcing organization equipping steward leaders for excellence in leadership. He is also a Senior Fellow of the Engstrom Institute.

Dr. Rodin is past president of the Christian Stewardship Association and was formerly the president of Eastern Baptist Theological Seminary in Philadelphia. He serves on the Boards of ChinaSource and the Evangelical Environmental Network.

He holds Master of Theology and Doctor of Philosophy degrees in Systematic Theology from the University of Aberdeen, Scotland.

Scott and his wife, Linda, reside in Spokane, Washington.

To order books or request for Dr. Rodin to speak go to:
www.kingdomlifepublishing.com

To order Scott Rodin's books
visit Kingdom Life Publishing at
www.kingdomlifepublishing.com

The Million-Dollar Dime

The Third Conversion

The Steward Leader

The Sower

The Four Gifts of the King

The Seven Deadly Sins of Christian Fundraising

Abundant Life

Stewards in the Kingdom